WHAT *IS* THIS?

FINDING DIRECTION WHEN LIFE'S STORMS LEAVE
YOU AND YOUR FAMILY SPEECHLESS

Michelle Karume

TRILOGY CHRISTIAN PUBLISHERS
Tustin, CA

Trilogy Christian Publishers
A Wholly Owned Subsidary of Trinity Broadcasting Network
2442 Michelle Drive Tustin, CA 92780

What Is This? Finding Direction When Life's Storms Leave You and Your Family Speechless

Rights Department, 2442 Michelle Drive, Tustin, CA 92780.

Trilogy Christian Publishing/TBN and colophon are trademarks of Trinity Broadcasting Network.

For information about special discounts for bulk purchases, please contact Trilogy Christian Publishing.

Trilogy Disclaimer: The views and content expressed in this book are those of the author and may not necessarily reflect the views and doctrine of Trilogy Christian Publishing or the Trinity Broadcasting Network.

Manufactured in the United States of America

10 9 8 7 6 5 4 3 2 1

Library of Congress Cataloging-in-Publication Data is available.

ISBN: 978-1-68556-683-8

E-ISBN: 978-1-68556-684-5

DEDICATION

To my mother, Lucy, and my brother, Njenga,
for always being there for me.
To all you, families, who choose to keep
fighting the storms of life—together!

ACKNOWLEDGEMENTS

I would like to thank my prayer team for steadfastly praying for this project from inception. I would also like to thank Trilogy Publishing for their dedication to spreading God's message across the world. I especially want to thank Mark Mingle, the acquisitions executive, who, from the beginning, ensured that all my questions were answered and that I had all pertinent documents.

My project manager, Jody Patton: thank you for your expertise on this project and for walking each step of the way with me. The layout artist and editorial team: thank you for bringing the creative vision of the project to life.

CONTENTS

INTRODUCTION

If you are like me, you understand that life can be challenging and that, as families and individuals, we all go through some things. However, no matter how much I understand that, I sure wish they were not so painful or, sometimes, so many. The ones that feel as if they have come out of nowhere are the ones I struggle with the most. I find myself asking, "What is this? Why does this happen to me? What is the point of this challenge? How will I make it through this?" I want to imagine the same is true for challenges faced by families. It could be one person who is front and center of the situation, but for the family members, this can be just as painful to have to see them go through it.

No matter how difficult the challenge I have faced, I always find myself looking for the road map on how to deal with it. I want to know how others dealt with similar situations; I want to know how to go through it effectively so that I can "pass the test." As a therapist, I have the honor of walking with people through their most trying times. Emotional pain is palpable, and the one thing they want to know is, "Dr. Michelle, how do I stop this pain?" "I will do anything," they say, "just tell me what to do." Now, because as therapists, we do not give advice, what I have found, however, is that walking alongside this family or individual is far more beneficial to the process of their healing than if I was to "tell them what to do." Giving them the effective tools is a priceless gift they get, for not only does it equip them for this season but for every other tough season they may go through. They complete sessions with a new packed bag of emotional tools. But if you do not have the right tools or the community to support you, then making it through becomes an arduous task. See, every storm is not wasted; every tear cried is not for nothing—it is all part of the bigger plan. Whereas the situation could truly be unfair and not right, God has a way of turning those dark moments into moments of light.

Time is another factor that plays into the challenges: they seem to take far much longer than I would appreciate. But this, too, I have learned is essential to building your character, deepening your faith, and developing you for greater blessings. Can I be honest with you? When someone would tell me that my character was being built or that my faith was being deepened, my response was, "Well, I didn't ask for a deeper faith or stronger character; I'm fine the way I am. We don't need to strengthen anything." Have you ever felt that way? Like, "My goodness, why does it have to be so hard" or "why does it feel like punishment to build this character? Surely, there can be another way to do it!" If you've ever felt this way, I hear you. However, let the next few weeks of this Bible study teach you more effective ways of handling those challenges. This way of thinking, I learned from my own experience, only delayed the process. I have since learned that the posture I take and the attitude I hold will determine how well I go through these challenges. I'm, by no means, an expert now, but I can shed light on a few ways of how to face the armies before you.

So, if you have ever wondered what to do as a family when going through a tough season or how to support your loved one dealing with a challenge, well, this Bible study is for you. In the next few weeks, we shall use the story of King Jehoshaphat to see how and what to do when we have been faced with a tough season. We will journey together using a road map that will equip us for today's and tomorrow's challenges.

You, God, are my God, earnestly I seek you; I thirst for you, my whole being longs for you, in a dry and parched land where there is no water.

Psalm 63:1

HOW TO GET THE MOST FROM THIS STUDY

This Bible study includes six weeks of material broken down by five days per week. You can do this study as a family, Bible study group, or personally.

Group Sessions

You can choose to do this study with your family, church-life group, or group of friends. Pick a day of the week and time that is consistent for the duration of the study. This helps give structure to the groups and creates emotional safety for its members. A suggested way to run the groups is as follows: each week, the group's members will do the following:

- read the book and watch the videos (if they are available) for each day of the week you are in,
- fill in all your responses in the blanks given in the book,
- meet with your group to have the study,
- be open to sharing and hearing from your group's members,
- have an open heart ready to hear from the Lord.

Tips for Group Leaders

The group facilitator opens the meeting with a prayer and sets the tone for the week's topic that you have all prepared for. Preparation will really help the group run smoothly. Review the material and study it for yourself. Anticipate questions and write some down. For the initial phase of the group, these questions are helpful in getting the group's members talking and acclimated with each other.

Pray for each member of the group and ask the Holy Spirit to use you as you facilitate the study.

Refreshments are always a great treat to have: they also set an intimate tone for new members.

Tips for Members

Prepare for your weekly group meeting by making sure you have completed all five days' material. The facilitator is exactly that—a facilitator, so full participation from you helps you get the most out of the study as you learn from each other and from God.

Personal Study

Each week has five days of Bible study and video series (if included with this study) to be accompanied with. Apply the activities and teachings to your personal life. The extra two days are good for reflection and worship as you look forward to the next week's study.

Additional stationery you will need for this study:

- your Bible,
- a journal for personal notes,
- pens, and
- highlighters.

Jehoshaphat Defeats Moab and Ammon

After this, the Moabites and Ammonites with some of the Meunites came to wage war against Jehoshaphat.

Some people came and told Jehoshaphat, "A vast army is coming against you from Edom, from the other side of the Dead Sea. It is already in Hazezon Tamar" (that is, En Gedi). Alarmed, Jehoshaphat resolved to inquire of the LORD, and he proclaimed a fast for all Judah. The people of Judah came together to seek help from the LORD; indeed, they came from every town in Judah to seek him.

Then Jehoshaphat stood up in the assembly of Judah and Jerusalem at the temple of the LORD in the front of the new courtyard and said:

"LORD, the God of our ancestors, are you not the God who is in heaven? You rule over all the kingdoms of the nations. Power and might are in your hand, and no one can withstand you. Our God, did you not drive out the inhabitants of this land before your people Israel and give it forever to the descendants of Abraham your friend? They have lived in it and have built in it a sanctuary for your Name, saying, 'If calamity comes upon us, whether the sword of judgment, or plague or famine, we will stand in your presence before this temple that bears your Name and will cry out to you in our distress, and you will hear us and save us.'

"But now here are men from Ammon, Moab and Mount Seir, whose territory you would not allow Israel to invade when they came from Egypt; so they turned away from them and did not destroy them. See how they are repaying us by coming to drive us out of the possession you gave us as an inheritance. Our God, will you not judge them? For we have no power to face this vast army that is attacking us. We do not know what to do, but our eyes are on you."

All the men of Judah, with their wives and children and little ones, stood there before the LORD.

Then the Spirit of the LORD came on Jahaziel son of Zechariah, the son of Benaiah, the son of Jeiel, the son of Mattaniah, a Levite and descendant of Asaph, as he stood in the assembly.

He said: "Listen, King Jehoshaphat and all who live in Judah and Jerusalem! This is what the LORD says to you: 'Do not be afraid or discouraged because of this vast army. For the battle is not yours, but God's. Tomorrow march down against them. They will be climbing up by the Pass of Ziz, and you will find them at the end of the gorge in the Desert of Jeruel. You will not have to fight this battle. Take up your positions; stand firm and see the deliverance the LORD will give you, Judah and Jerusalem. Do not be afraid; do not be discouraged. Go out to face them tomorrow, and the LORD will be with you.'"

Jehoshaphat bowed down with his face to the ground, and all the people of Judah and Jerusalem fell down in worship before the LORD. Then some Levites from the Kohathites and Korahites stood up and praised the LORD, the God of Israel, with a very loud voice.

Early in the morning they left for the Desert of Tekoa. As they set out, Jehoshaphat stood and said, "Listen to me, Judah and people of Jerusalem! Have faith in the LORD your God and you will be upheld; have faith in his prophets and you will be successful." After consulting the people, Jehoshaphat appointed men to sing to the LORD and to praise him for the splendor of his holiness as they went out at the head of the army, saying: "Give thanks to the LORD, for his love endures forever."

As they began to sing and praise, the LORD set ambushes against the men of Ammon and Moab and Mount Seir who were invading Judah, and they were defeated. The Ammonites and Moabites rose up against the men from Mount Seir to destroy and annihilate them. After they finished slaughtering the men from Seir, they helped to destroy one another.

When the men of Judah came to the place that overlooks the desert and looked toward the vast army, they saw only dead bodies lying on the ground; no one had escaped. So Jehoshaphat and his men went to carry off their plunder, and they found among them a great amount of equipment and clothing and also articles of value—more than they could take away. There was so much plunder that it took three days to collect it.

On the fourth day they assembled in the Valley of Beracah, where they praised the LORD. This is why it is called the Valley of Beracah to this day.

Then, led by Jehoshaphat, all the men of Judah and Jerusalem returned joyfully to Jerusalem, for the LORD had given them cause to rejoice over their enemies. They entered Jerusalem and went to the temple of the LORD with harps and lyres and trumpets.

The fear of God came on all the surrounding kingdoms when they heard how the LORD had fought against the enemies of Israel. And the kingdom of Jehoshaphat was at peace, for his God had given him rest on every side.

2 Chronicles 20:1–30

INQUIRE
OF THE LORD

AFTER THIS

As indicated in the introduction, we are going to use the story of King Jehoshaphat as a guide to teach ourselves how to manage the storms of life. These six weeks we shall spend in this study shall teach us God's way of fighting.

I knew that I was to write a Bible study but did not know what story or character or theme to use. The story of King Jehoshaphat is found in 2 Chronicles 20:1–30. This has always been my favorite story in the Bible, so you can imagine how elated I was when God made it clear that this was the anchor story for the study, that it was this story that God wanted us to use to better equip us as we battle the quick and small everyday challenges! We shall go verse by verse, extrapolating the insights and teachings that they each have. This story does not waste time; it goes straight into business.

This Bible chapter of King Jehoshaphat reminds me of a story I read once about the eagle and the raven. The story told of how strategic the eagle was to get the raven off its back. See, when the eagle would take flight, the raven would hop on its back and annoyingly peck at it. I would imagine this weighed the eagle down, not to mention how annoying it must have been. However, the eagle used its wisdom, and instead of fighting back the way one would think it should, by probably trying to shake the raven off, the eagle did something very interesting. The eagle did not waste its energy on the raven; instead, it flew higher. See, the higher altitudes are tough for ravens: they cannot breathe, and so the higher the eagle flew, the tougher it got for the raven, eventually falling off on its own. Strategy: the eagle could have chosen to react but, instead, used its gift of being able to fly in high altitudes.

The story of King Jehoshaphat reminds me of the eagle. God uses such a profound strategy to conquer the armies that are fast approaching the king and his people. From 2 Chronicles 20:1, we already get our first teaching and insight. We will need to review 2 Chronicles 18–19 to understand the insight in today's first lesson fully. But to start, turn to and read 2 Chronicles 20:1.

Record 2 Chronicles 20:1 here:

_____

_____

_____

_____

_____

_____

Now, circle the words "after this" in the verse above.

Isn't it interesting that when life is going well, you've been making good choices, perhaps you've even received a promotion at work, or your family is doing well, that someone or something comes to try and destroy that? I have a comical theory about how the enemy works. I call it "running the enemy's errands." I believe that every morning, the enemy looks for people to run its errands. So, it asks, "Who [could also be a thing, an illness, a situation, a person] will go and disrupt [your name here]'s day today?" And then people or illnesses, calamities, etc., raise their hands to run these errands. This year, for example, the COVID-19 virus has raised its hand, and with it, it has brought on others: storms that the globe continues to suffer, political unrest in some countries, invasion of locusts, floods so heavy that they have wiped out homes, hurricanes, loss of jobs, and economic struggles to name a few.

Unfortunately, in our personal lives, these "hand-raisers" could sometimes be those close to us like friends, coworkers, family members, or associates at organizations like the bank or the dry cleaner or the grocery store. Earlier I mentioned we would need to go back to 2 Chronicles 18 and 19 so as to have a better understanding of what had happened before. It will make sense why we circled "after this" above in just a moment.

So, turn to 2 Chronicles 18:28–32 and 2 Chronicles 19:4–11 in your Bible. Two significant things had just happened before the armies started coming after Jehoshaphat.

The first is that Jehoshaphat, king of Judah, in chapter 18, is tricked by the king of Israel to wear his robe while he disguises himself. "When the chariot commanders saw Jehoshaphat, they thought, 'This is the king of Israel.' So they turned to attack him, but Jehoshaphat cried out, and the LORD helped him" (2 Chronicles 18:31). So, the threat to King Jehoshaphat came after he had cried out to God but also after he had appointed judges in the land (2 Chronicles 19:4–11), which was the second thing that had taken place. Whenever countries appoint judges, it is a big deal. People celebrate, as these are very high positions in society. I imagine family members were so proud of their loved ones being selected as judges, priests, and heads of Israelite families for their community. So, this was a time of celebration in their community; King Jehoshaphat had done a good thing because he had appointed not only judges but also priests and heads of Israelite families to administer the law of the Lord, who would settle all disputes. This was a great achievement!

Using 2 Chronicles 19:6–7, write down what the king told them:

"Consider carefully,

_____

_____

_____

_____

_____

_____

_____."

Using 2 Chronicles 19:9–10, write down the orders he also gave them:

_____

_____

_____

_____

_____

_____

So, new judges, priests, and heads of Israelite families have been appointed to ensure, basically, that justice in the land is served.

Then here come the hand-raisers, yup, ready to run the enemy's errands. Complete this sentence from 2 Chronicles 20:1. Who are the hand-raisers?

The _____ and _____ with some of the _____ came (raised their hands) to make war on Jehoshaphat.

You may be going through a challenge right now where things are just coming at you, whether it's your health, finances, bills piling up, family challenges, personal challenges, and you just can't seem to catch a break.

In Psalm 83:2, we see the psalmist crying out to God because the "enemies are astir" and "your foes rear their heads." When going through the storms of life, we all reach a place where it gets to be "too much," where we grow faint, but God calls on us to cry out to Him, as we see demonstrated in Psalm 83:1 where it reads, "O God, do not keep silent; be not quiet, O God, be not still."

In Psalm 83:6–8, we also see the psalmist writing down the list of enemies coming against him.

List down the challenges you are facing today.

_____

_____

_____

_____

_____

_____

_____

In reference to 2 Chronicles 20:1, what was the "after this" moment you had gone through? What good things were happening before the challenge(s) you are facing came? What was life like before the challenge(s) listed above came?

_____

_____

_____

_____

_____

If you feel overwhelmed, perhaps the enemy has you fearful either for yourself or a loved one, and you don't know how to fight these battles, this Bible study is for you! Its aim is to help you discover how, like the eagle, to fight these challenges the right way...God's way.

As we go through these six weeks of study, we will be using the story of King Jehoshaphat in 2 Chronicles 20 to show us how God's sovereign love for us will give us "rest on every side" (as is written in 2 Chronicles 20:30, but let's not get ahead of ourselves: we shall glean from that verse in week six) when our families and we are faced with challenges. We are also going to learn how equipped we are because we have Jesus on our side. We shall learn how to be discerning of the things of God and those not of Him.

What Are You Most Grateful for Today?

At the end of each day, I will ask you to write down what you are most grateful for on that day. See, when you are in the middle of a war, it is hard to see anything good on that day. The enemy is very good at making us see things from the negative and ensuring we do not notice anything positive. By writing down what you are grateful for each day, you begin to see the blessings that each day has, even in the midst of the storm. You will choose five things you are most grateful for. You know you are doing this exercise correctly when you literally split hairs on the things you are grateful for.

For example: "I am grateful for my family." Whereas this is a good thing, for the purposes of the effectiveness of this exercise, this is too broad, and by day three, the task will only get redundant and thus not effective. Instead, here is the correct way to give gratitude for your family: you can say, "Today, I am most grateful for my cousin John who called to check on me. I have not spoken to him in a while, and it was great hearing from him." Now, this is more personal, more precise about what it was about your family that you were grateful for on that day.

So, what five things are you grateful for today? (I find it easier to do this at the end of the day so that I have more data to choose from.)

_____

_____

_____

_____

_____

_____

Conclude today's study by seeking God in prayer, letting Him know the challenges you are facing, and asking Him to help you fight this battle, for, without Him, it is impossible to win. Also, thank Him that even despite these storms, there are still things to be grateful for.

A VAST ARMY IS COMING

I'm sure you've heard the phrase "when it rains, it pours." Several years ago, this phrase became true for my family and me. I mean, everything we could imagine going wrong did. I took ill and ended up needing surgery. This was a routine surgery in that it is very common, and the healing process is usually about two weeks.

I remember having a bit of a push and pull with the doctor regarding these two weeks. Given that I am a professor, I could not foresee not being in class. So, I was asking for five days off, given that the beginning of the semester was when I would be in recovery. Well, the storms came, and five days off or two weeks off became a moot point. I found myself in the middle of a medical error, which led to loss of blood in surgery and what ended up being a yearlong fight for my life. The complications from the medical error had brought on their own set of challenges affecting other organs in my body. The time before this that I had spent a night in the hospital was the day I was born. Talk about zero to hundred.

So, even being in the hospital as a patient was new for me. That term, "patient," felt foreign. As a medical family therapist, I spend a lot of time in the hospital, visiting patients and their families. Never had I been in the reserve role. The same year, not just my nuclear family but the extended family were under attack in varying ways. We lost loved ones that year; other family members took ill as well; family challenges were on the rise. My mother was in an accident that severed her shoulder, which led to her needing emergency surgery. Not to mention this accident happened on the arm that had previously been injured years ago. Our families fell on hard financial times where making ends meet seemed impossible. Businesses plummeted; employment opportunities were not coming to fruition—should I go on? I mean, that year was one for the books. The level of despair that gripped my family was harrowing. We all walked about, fearful of the next phone call because we could hardly catch a break and all news seemed like bad news.

I can tell you this: there were lots of hands being raised that year for my family. It rained; it poured; it stormed; it hurricaned (I just made up that word, but you get what I mean). One year has never felt so long for us. But the prayers remained constant. As the armies came, we stood; even with tears, fatigue, and fear, we stood. We had no other choice: only God could get us out of these situations. I recall moments when I could not even pray: the words would fail me, but I took comfort in knowing that my sigh or cry spoke volumes to Jesus, and He understood exactly what I was going through. It was amazing to me that even when my words failed, Jesus was right there with my family and me. Let's see how armies were coming at King Jehoshaphat and his people as well in verse 2.

Read 2 Chronicles 20:2 and write it down in this section.

_____

_____

Similarly, read Genesis 14:7. In this chapter, we see an account of another war situation where armies came and conquered the territory of the Amalekites. This was the way in which they knew to deal with challenges—they went into war. Whereas this is one way to manage disputes among countries, we, in our own personal lives, have challenges as well that we need to conquer.

In today's chapter (2 Chronicles 20:2), we see that King Jehoshaphat was given a warning by "some men." They came to warn him of the armies coming, the direction they were coming from, and how far they had reached. Write down any warning signs you received about the challenges you are facing. Did anyone give you fair warning?

_____
_____
_____
_____

Your answer above could be *no*, you did not receive any warning, and if you are like me, you sure would want a warning before a challenge so you can suit up. However, I have also learned that many a time, we do receive a gut feeling of sorts, which we don't always pay attention to.

Write down situations when you did get a gut feeling about something, ignored it, and the worst came to pass.

_____
_____
_____
_____

Life has become fast-paced, and with that, we sometimes miss out on the important things that happen in the stillness of moments. Psalm 46:10 reads, "Be still and know that I am God." *Be still*. God loves us so much that He wants us not to worry but to trust Him and His ways. Could it be that we need to be still so as to hear of some warnings? But in order to be able to hear God, we need to be still. He oftentimes is the one giving us the warning signs, but in the noise of life, we can miss hearing Him.

In what ways do you need to slow down so that you can hear God this week? Write these ways down and share them in the group.

_____

_____

_____

_____

_____

What does being still look like for you?

_____

_____

_____

_____

_____

As we conclude today's study, purpose yourself this week to be still and spend some time with God. You may have been warned of the vast army that's coming, but God commands us to *be still*.

What five things are you most grateful for today?

_____

_____

_____

_____

_____

_____

_____

_____

_____

_____

WE MEAN BUSINESS

Yesterday we learned about the importance of being still so as to be able to hear God. Today we are learning about another specific profound fighting strategy, *fasting*. When I was a swimmer, our coaches would always prepare us well for our swim meets. We would practice before classes in the morning, at lunchtime, and also in the evenings before going home. The closer we got to the day of the meets, the more intense the practice got. Bigger swim meets constituted even more preparation.

You knew a team meant business when they would come with their cheerleaders, when they would get to the event much earlier to do some laps in the pool, when school would allow us to skip a class or two for us to have some extra swimming training. This was when your personal swim time meant everything, and you wanted to know what the fastest swimmer's time was so as to set a record for yourself.

I always kept my best bathing suit for the swim meets. I had one pair of swimming goggles that I took extra care of because of the meets. The swimming caps were notorious for melting in the heat, tearing, or better still, letting water in. Before swim meets, we all made sure to line the cap with baby powder so as to avoid the melting and, when possible, would carry two or three caps, just in case. Then there was your research. For a swimmer, it was imperative to do research on the sport. We studied swimming techniques and immersed ourselves in all things swimming. We meant business!

Let us turn to 2 Chronicles 20:3 and see how serious things got in the community. Write down, word for word, the verse of 2 Chronicles 20:3.

_____

_____

_____

_____

What did King Jehoshaphat proclaim?

_____

_____

_____

_____

Before proclaiming the fast, was he alarmed?

_____

_____

_____

_____

It gives comfort to know that even a king can be alarmed at the sight of a vast army. So, even though it is scary to receive that termination from our job or a report from the doctor or have a family member who is struggling with something, we have hope that there is one in whom we can anchor ourselves. Oftentimes, however, when these challenges come, we contact our loved ones first, when we should contact Jesus first. What did King Jehoshaphat resolve to do immediately?

He resolved to _____

_____.

There is power in going to God first; turn to Matthew 6:33 and write it down here:

_____

_____

_____

_____

List down examples of challenges you faced in the past when you sought God first, before anyone else.

_____

_____

_____

_____

What was different about those times versus when challenges came and you did not seek God first?

_____

_____

_____

_____

The Power of Fasting

When it comes to fasting, we see countless times in the Bible when people took to fasting. Take, for example, Ezra 8:23. Here we see Ezra preparing for a trip, and before he departs, he calls for a fast. Earlier, we saw King Jehoshaphat do the same thing; he proclaimed a fast to petition God for direction. There are countless reasons for and benefits of fasting. In these two examples, we see three important reasons why we should fast:

1. to seek guidance: King Jehoshaphat does this;

2. to strengthen prayer: we see this in the case of Ezra;

3. to seek protection and deliverance: we see this with King Jehoshaphat. Once he was informed about the armies approaching him, he immediately declared a fast. He could have fasted alone, but notice that he chose for his people to fast with him. Put a pin on that because we shall explore this tomorrow as we list more reasons why people fast.

Another reason why fasting is important is documented in Nehemiah 1:4. We learn that fasting is a strategy Jesus has given us as our battle tool. Write out this verse here in the space provided and underline the reasons why you think Nehemiah went into fasting.

_____

_____

_____

_____

So, a fifth reason why fasting is important is that it allows us to express grief and despair. Nehemiah had just been given a report about the great trouble in Jerusalem, and for some days, he mourned and fasted before God. Fasting is a powerful key that unlocks peace, strategy, and plans for navigating the challenges of life.

You may be reading this and perhaps, for medical reasons, may not be able to fast. Having gone through medical challenges in the past, I, too, could not fast. Not to worry: tomorrow, we take a look at how you can still have the same effects of fasting when you yourself cannot do it.

Let's read the following verses out loud to hear of more accounts where fasting was chosen by God's people for various reasons, all culminating in them showing that they meant business. Beside each verse, write down why the people were fasting. You may need to read more of the stories than just the verse to get the full meaning of what was going on. Spend some time understanding the stories below and jot down the reasons you think these people fasted in each case.

Fill in the column on the right.

Verses	Reason for Fasting
Isaiah 58:6	
Jeremiah 36:9	
Daniel 9:3	
Joel 1:14 and 2:15	
Jonah 3:5, 7	

What do you notice about the positions or situations the people were in that resulted in them going into fasting and praying?

_____

_____

_____

_____

List down the reasons you have learned in today's study of how fasting is a crucial strategy when the armies of life are coming at you.

_____
_____
_____
_____
_____
_____
_____

As we conclude, underline one of the above reasons why *you* would need to fast or have needed to fast in the past.

What five things are you most grateful for today?

_____
_____
_____
_____
_____
_____
_____

POWER IN NUMBERS

If you've ever had to sign a petition at work for something you were advocating for, you know that the power was in the numbers: the more people you got to sign the petition, the higher the chances for the plan to be passed. The same concept applies when it comes to voting: the more votes the candidate has, the higher the chances for her or him to win the election. There is power in numbers.

I tend to think that, similarly, when an individual has support to cheer and encourage them through an event in their life, they actually do better due to this support. It gives them the morale they need to make it through, even when losing; it gives them the strength to complete the race. I think of Olympic athletes. If you've ever watched a race from start to finish, you notice key players in the race other than the athletes: there's the judging panel, the coaches, the camera crew, and lots of other officials. But then, there are the cheering crowds! When you look at the sidelines, you see flags, family members, fellow countrymen and women, supporters—all geared up to cheer their candidate. The anticipation before each race is palpable. The athletes gain even more strength to complete the race when they have their supporters encouraging them. It gives them the extra wind to run the course and not give up even though sometimes, I'm sure, they are so tired, but they keep pushing. My favorite scene is when the cameras pan to the family—what emotion and desperation it must be to see their family member finish strong!

In the moments between the start and the finish, the cheers rise to the skies with melodic sounds. They sing in unison the songs of inspiration. Music unites us; cheering for a loved one does the same. The louder the music, the harder the athlete pushes. He can hear them; he can feel the wind against his tired limbs, but he keeps pushing.

Suppose this athlete was a world record holder; I have no doubt in my mind that even if he ran without anyone cheering, he probably would still finish the race. But it would be an arduous task. The power in the numbers is the wind in his sails. The encouragement pushes him further; it gives him strength, perhaps even when he wants nothing else but to stop.

Like athletes, we all need people to encourage us when a challenge is before us. Yesterday, I said that you may not be in a position to fast and pray for yourself. But it is here where the power in your numbers comes in. Your cheering squad can help push you through. Gather your community, lean on them to pray you through.

I remember the time when I took ill and the doctors had me on a specific diet so as to stop some reactions I was experiencing. This was a tough season, certainly not one I had prepared for, like in the case of athletes. I remember the days got so tough, nights got really dark, but there was a community of saints who were praying for me constantly. I could not have done this without them. Due to the very strict dietary restrictions, fasting was not an option for me, but my friends fasted on my behalf.

We see an example of this type of support in the book of Esther: Mordecai posed a challenge to her that only she could deliver, but it had never been done, and those who tried were put to death (Esther 4:11). Turn to this chapter and read verse 11.

Chances are the situation before you is an uphill battle, and so, in order for you to "touch the hem of His garment," as is in the story of the woman with the issue of blood in Matthew 9:20 (KJV), you need to do more in addition to your regular prayers. Turn to this story in Matthew 9. You will see that there were so many people surrounding Jesus, but she pushed through them all. In my situation, I also needed to up the ante. My body was weak; my spirit was down. I could not do it alone, so I sought my community to fast.

In the space below, write down Esther 4:16.

_____

_____

_____

_____

Circle "Go, gather together all the Jews who are in Susa, and fast for me." She required protection, and Mordecai required deliverance. So, Mordecai and the Jews gathered and did exactly that—they prayed and fasted for Esther to find favor with the king.

What part of your situation currently looks impossible? Write it down here.

_____

_____

_____

_____

Who among your friends and family can you call on to pray and fast for you? Write their names here.

_____

_____

_____

_____

If you are in a situation where you don't have a strong community, maybe you are new to your Bible study, reach out to the leader of the study and let them know that you need support. There is nothing wrong with asking for help. We all need to, from time to time.

Also, I know that many churches have prayer teams that stand with others during difficult times. Maybe you can reach out to one of those. One thing that helped me was listening to sermons that spoke to my situation. That's another way to get support. Know this: even if you do not have a community (yet), Jesus is with you, and He is the majority, so do not be discouraged.

In 2 Chronicles 20:4, it reads, "The people of Judah came together to seek help from the LORD: indeed they came from every town in Judah to seek him."

They all came with one challenge in mind: the army that was fast approaching the king, and even though the enemies came to wage war against Jehoshaphat (2 Chronicles 20:1), the people of Judah had the power of numbers: all of them, "from every town," seeking the Lord on the king's behalf. I don't know about you, but for me, this is exciting and encouraging at the same time. When the storms of life get tough, your loved ones can stand in the gap for you! Jesus, in His precious nature, knew that life could get tough for us and that we would need others to pray us through those seasons.

As we conclude today's session, I hope you are encouraged that you need not go through this situation alone and that it is okay to have days when you are down and cannot petition God for yourself.

Also, if you know of someone going through a tough time, why don't you reach out this week and let them know that you are praying for them and perhaps could even fast for them? Sometimes, we should be like the people of Judah, seeking God for help for a loved one.

Who can you encourage this week?

Name: _____

What five things are you most grateful for today?

_____

_____

_____

_____

_____

_____

You don't have to fast only food; you can fast other things. The point is to pick something where you will feel the pinch. If the internet or television are things you have a great affinity for, then fast that.

LEADERSHIP

I'd imagine that with the support he received from the people of Judah, Jehoshaphat was now able to stand in front of his people and lead them in prayer. I often see this when people are making a public announcement; they have "their people" standing behind them in support as they convey their message. For a leader, it often poses a challenge to be going through stuff— more so than people would imagine—because there are such high expectations of them.

Even when they are faced with a challenge, people still look to them for direction. In 2 Chronicles 20:5, however, we see a different kind of leadership being demonstrated. King Jehoshaphat, in front of his people, as we shall see tomorrow, gets vulnerable before God. In his time of weakness, he stood in front of his people and still taught them life lessons on what needed to be done.

There is something about the metaphor of "to stand." Standing, even when the reports say otherwise, even when the bank account is low, even when that child is still straying away from the ways of the Lord, even when you yourself want to give up on that business but stand and continue leading.

The posture you take while going through this challenge can either make or break the situation. Jehoshaphat took an upright position of standing. This sets the tone for those around you and those coming against you. If you take a victim role, then the enemy sees the weak places to attack. This is not to say that you cannot be down or have bad days, no; it's to say that only "your people" should see that side of you, not the enemy.

There is a theme we see in 2 Chronicles 20: when leaders seek the Lord, you can expect that He will do great things for them and their people. So, whatever leadership position you may hold, seek the Lord regarding the army you are facing.

2 Chronicles 20:5

Where did Jehoshaphat stand?

_____

_____

At what location did he stand?

_____

_____

In front of what?

_____

_____

It sounds to me as if he was very strategic about his position. He did not just stand anywhere and in front of just anyone.

Those you choose to stand in front of and lead or share your journey with must have earned the right to hear your story.

25

In this situation, you are the leader: set the precedence but ensure to allow your community (that you have selected) to support you. Closing off and isolating only makes things worse.

In day-to-day practical living, you stand by honoring God, being obedient to His Word, and putting Him first place in your life. So, continue being planted in your church, paying your tithes, serving in your community, being a blessing to your family, working diligently at work, etc. Don't stop honoring God as you fight this battle.

In what ways have you stopped honoring God due to the disruption this challenge has caused? Write those things down here:

_____

_____

_____

_____

_____

It helps to identify a scripture or two and meditate on these verses as you deal with the challenge. I used Post-it Notes, wrote encouraging scriptures that ministered to my situation, and placed them everywhere in my room so I would be reminded of what it was I was standing on. I was reminded of the truth regardless of what the situation looked like. One scripture that really helped me when fear gripped my heart was 2 Timothy 1:7, "For God did not give us a spirit of timidity, but a spirit of power, of love and of self-discipline." I repeated this verse over and over again. Writing down those scriptures was me taking command of the situation and letting the enemy know who was and still is in charge!

Write down a few scriptures here to help you get started.

_____

_____

_____

_____

What aspects of your situation do you need to take the leadership role in? Do you need to speak up and voice your opinion at
work? Do you need to advocate for yourself with the doctors?
Do you need to give direction to your community on how to go
in this situation as they stand with you? Whatever is the case
you may be in, write these aspects down here and use this list
as a guide for yourself.

_____

_____

_____

_____

Part of being a leader is to delegate roles, as it is easy to get
overwhelmed. Read Exodus 18:21. What sort of men and wom-
en does it say to select?

Men and women who?

_____

_____

Who are?

_____

_____

And who?

_____

_____

As we conclude this week's study, let's see how we can lighten the burden you are facing.

When managing all the stress that my family and I were going through, I found it really helped to delegate tasks that we ourselves could not handle at the time. But selecting the people was also a crucial task, as we see demonstrated by Jethro in Exodus 18 above.

Delegating can be hard for people (especially when you are going through difficulties); however, I think it makes for better leadership so that you can even out the tasks and accomplish more in less time and with better quality (and not at the price of one person).

What tasks can you delegate and to whom? Fill out the table to help you manage the, perhaps, pile of stuff that needs attention during this time.

Task	Delegate to

What five things are you most grateful for today?

_____

_____

_____

_____

_____

_____

_____

PETITION THROUGH PRAYER

WHO HOLDS THE POWER?

And said; O LORD, God of our fathers, are you not the God who is in heaven? You rule over all the kingdoms of the nations. Power and might are in your hand, and no one can withstand you.

2 Chronicles 20:6

We are now in verse 6 of our theme story of King Jehoshaphat and his people. And in today's study, we learn about who holds the power.

As I sat writing this chapter, I paused to hear what sounded like the ocean, like waves moving up and down the seashore. I was curious because I was nowhere near the beach, but to my surprise, it was the wind. The winds were so strong on that day, and because I was sitting on a balcony that was on the second floor, my view was of the top of the trees swaying majestically to and fro. I was taken aback by how strong the winds were, how blue the sky was with not a cloud in sight. The leaves of the trees were dancing to the tune of the winds; the birds were chirping louder than usual. I guess the winds were causing them to be unsettled. In a far-off distance, I could hear some cars, some music from nearby restaurants, but the loudest sound was the wind.

It was like an orchestra in the sky, accompanied by the backdrop of the sun. The trees looked melodic, enjoying the moment, but not long after, the wind settled, and the trees began to calm down. Not immediately, though, but slowly; it was as though someone was turning down the dial, and before I knew it, there came another gush of wind, and up the trees, the branches went, and the song of the wind started again. All this was because of the wind, which I could hear very clearly, could not see but knew it was there. Some notes of the wind sounded like whistles and chimes, and other times, the sound would become two-toned, the sound of the rustling plus whistles, which were formed by the pine trees. What an experience. The trees were not swaying in the same direction. It was as if the winds were coming from every direction, making circular motions in how the trees swayed. What power!

I sat there and was reminded of Psalm 78:26, "He let loose the east wind from the heavens, and led forth the south wind by His power" (hereinafter, emphasis mine). You know, scientists may have tried but certainly cannot make winds blow this way, the sun rise and set, rainbows form in the sky, and ocean tides come in and out as they do; only God holds the power to do so!

As the winds in my view took over the heavens, I was also reminded of Job 37, where Eliud is encouraging Job, reminding him of God's majestic power. It is in Job 32 that we are introduced to Eliud, Job's youngest friend. He is said to have been self-assertive and vocal. But not going too much into Eliud himself, I want to bring your attention to Job 37.

Let's read Job 37:1–24.

Using a few verses in this chapter just to highlight God's power, fill in the blanks below:

Verses 3–8, 11–12: "He unleashes his lightning beneath the whole heaven and sends it to the ends of the earth. After that comes the sound of his roar; he thunders with _____ _____. When his voice resounds, he holds nothing back. _____ _____ he does great things _____ _____. He says to the snow, '_____,' and to the rain shower, 'Be a mighty downpour.' So that all men he has made may_____, he stops every man from his labor. The animals take cover, they _____ _____. [...] He loads the cloud with moisture; he scatters his lightning through them. At his direction they swirl around over the face of the whole earth to do whatever he commands them to do."

Wow, what a great God. Such power. I think about the days it rains heavily, and we have to run for shelter; we have to plan how to get home because the roads will be backed up due to the rains and traffic. Friend, be encouraged that this God who says to the snow "fall," and it falls, is *still* at work. Your situation may seem impossible to you but not to God.

Which verses from Job 37:1–24 stood out to you? Write them down here and commit them to memory as you go through this week.

_____
_____
_____
_____
_____
_____

Let's look at 2 Chronicles 20:6 again. In this verse, we see King Jehoshaphat asking rhetorical questions to God. It is not so much to be redundant but to emphasize the situation he has found himself in. He needs to remind himself and his people who, in fact, holds the power. Did you notice that the word "hand" is singular? With one hand, God can do all these things—*one hand*. I mean, two would have been impressive, but *one*? Now, that's power!

It is very easy to look at your situations and to science or logic and conclude that there is no way out of them: looking at the medical results, looking at the job situation, looking at the family dysfunction. It's easy to be caught up in following or looking to those situations for the answers.

When we think about the eagle, the eagle makes a choice; he chooses to fly higher, rise above the situation, and get to greater heights. In the same way, when choosing to look to Jesus rather than to those around you, you may find it's an irrational decision to make. Besides, "the doctor said," "the employer said," "the bank statement shows"—whereas that may be true, it's not what Jesus has said.

He holds the power! Write it on another sticky note and add it to the others in nice big, bold letters: *Jesus holds the power.*

Add to the list below the situations that you are dealing with and, beside them, write the words *"Jesus holds the power!"*

For example:
- My school tuition—*Jesus holds the power!*
- My employment status—*Jesus holds the power!*
- My health and medical report—*Jesus holds the power!*

_____

_____

_____

_____

_____

It may be impossible for you, but it is not impossible for God. Let's look at other scriptures that remind us of who is in control.

Read the following scriptures:
- Matthew 6:9
- Deuteronomy 4:39
- 1 Chronicles 29:11–12
- 2 Chronicles 25:8
- Job 25:2, 41:10, 42:2
- Isaiah 14:27
- Jeremiah 32:27, 49:19

It might seem as if God has forgotten you, for you have cried out, but nothing seems to change. God has not forgotten about you. God's timing and our timings are usually very different. But instead of focusing on the time lapse or the state of the situation, look to Him who holds the power and be encouraged.

You may ask, "But how exactly should I do that?"

Through your words. Speak life into your situation, remind yourself that you are courageous, you are strong, you are protected, you are loved, and you are able. Words are very powerful.

In the list of scriptures you just read above, is there one that stood out for you? Write it down here and apply it to your life and what you are currently facing. Speak words of life and encouragement, words that counter the grim situation that you are in...regardless of how you feel. Speak those words into existence.

_____

_____

_____

_____

_____

As a reminder, write down Jeremiah 32:27 and remember that *nothing is impossible or too hard for God.*

_____

_____

_____

_____

_____

Today's verse reminds us, "[...] and no one can withstand you" (2 Chronicles 20:6). As we conclude today, let this last part of 2 Chronicles 20:6 sink into your spirit: that there is no situation that can withstand God, none! Hold onto God's words with confidence, for *He holds the power!*

What are you most grateful for today? List down five things.

_____

_____

_____

_____

_____

_____

CONFIDENCE IN GOD

When I was younger, I really enjoyed sports: I swam, as you saw earlier, and I also played field hockey. My mother would come for most, if not all, of my meets and would cheer me on. One hockey game was going to be quite a challenge, given the team we were playing. My mother, like in every other game, told me that I was good, that I could do well in the game. Regardless of how I felt—scared, unsure, or nervous—I knew deep down that I would play well, not because of how I felt but because Mom said I would. I was more confident in her words than in my ability.

The game started, and I held onto Mom's words. I gave that game my all, and who would have known that it was going to be my best game? I did my personal best that day. Why? Because I believed in one higher than me, Mom.

Confidence is like a superpower. No matter how the situation may look, it may seem grim, but you stand on God's Word, unshakeable and sure.

Today we move to verse 7 of 2 Chronicles 20. In this verse, we shall learn about how confidence in God is part of the strategy when managing the stress before you. King Jehoshaphat prayed in recognition of God's past victories, so he knew that if God had done it before, then called upon, He could do it again.

Before we get to the verse, let's look at other scriptures that demonstrate what role confidence plays in your fight.

Write down these three scriptures below:

Genesis 12:7

_____
_____
_____
_____
_____
_____
_____

Isaiah 41:3–4, 13–14

_____
_____
_____
_____
_____
_____
_____

James 2:23–24

_____
_____
_____
_____
_____
_____

In summary, what are the things in these scriptures that God says He would do or give these people?

_____

_____

_____

_____

_____

_____

_____

When you read James 2:23–24, you notice that the tone of voice God uses is specific. What tone would you allocate to these two verses when He was declaring to them what He would do for them? (For example, is it a suggestive tone or a persuasive one?)

_____

_____

_____

_____

_____

_____

_____

How does Abram show his confidence in God in Genesis 12:7?

_____

_____

_____

_____

_____

What does God confidently state that He has done in Isaiah 41:3–4?

_____

_____

_____

_____

_____

_____

What does God say He will do for you in Isaiah 41:13–14?

_____

_____

_____

_____

_____

_____

Isn't that amazing and so reassuring of Jesus that He will take you by your right hand (visualize that) and then comfort you by saying, "Do not fear"? He doesn't suggest that you don't fear but commands—with surety and confidence.

In relationship to 2 Chronicles 20:7, King Jehoshaphat is highlighting a situation where God said He was going to give the land to Abraham's descendants forever. It sounds like the king is reminding God of the things He has done, but since God needs no reminder, these are more of rhetorical questions. The king is trying to highlight that when God says He will do something, He does it.

To emphasize this point, read these scriptures:

In Isaiah 55:11, God says, "So is my word that goes out from my mouth; it will not return to me empty, but will accomplish what I desire and achieve the purpose for which I sent it." Be confident in His Word and what *He* says about you, not what the situation says about you.

Philippians 1:6 reads, "Being confident of this, that he who began a good work in you will carry it on to completion until the day of Christ Jesus."

Do you remember a time when God said He was going to do something in your life and did it? Jot it down here. What did that feel like?

_____

_____

_____

_____

_____

_____

_____

Remember this:

"For the LORD will be your confidence and will keep your foot from being snared" (Proverbs 3:26).

"The LORD will be your everlasting light, and your days of sorrow will end" (Isaiah 60:20).

As we conclude today's study, in what ways can you choose to be confident in God this week? Find a scripture to stand on.

_____

_____

_____

_____

_____

What five things are you most grateful for today?

_____

_____

_____

_____

_____

SANCTUARY

Is there a place you go to and sit and be alone with God? One place that feels safe, peaceful, and enjoyable? Whereas I can name two or three for me: my favorite is my car, yup! Sitting in my car—there is something about it that makes me feel safe and protected. Whenever I can, I like to sit in my car and be alone and quiet, not necessarily doing anything but being quiet. It's also the place I like to go and think and gather my thoughts, make decisions. I can sit in my car for several hours, just thinking, people watching, praying; it's my sanctuary. I imagine it's like a prayer room or prayer closet that some people have. It's the place where everything makes sense. All around me, I can see there is movement and noise from other cars passing by, people walking to and from their cars in the parking lot, people talking; stuff is happening. But inside the car, there is a stillness, a quietness that is so calming, where the noise gets silenced and your voice and thoughts are privileged.

When the people of Israel in 2 Chronicles 20:8 built the sanctuary in the land the Lord had given them, I would imagine it felt safe once they had it there. The Bible says they build it for His name.

When the lights became dark for me, having a sanctuary—be it my office, my room, or my car—gave me a place to *just* be, to cry if I needed to, to laugh at things I remembered that cracked me up, to daydream when my mind wondered, to wish and hope in a way that felt peaceful and safe.

Where is your sanctuary?

_____

_____

_____

_____

_____

_____

When Solomon finished building the temple for the Lord, he dedicated it. In 2 Chronicles 6:20, he makes two requests of God. What are they? Write them here.

1) _____

_____

_____

_____

_____

2) _____

_____

_____

_____

That place that you go to be alone with God—dedicate it to the Lord, asking Him to "hear the supplications of your servant [you]" (2 Chronicles 6:21, text in brackets mine) just as Solomon did.

Why do you think the people of Israel built a sanctuary?

_____

_____

_____

_____

_____

What does Exodus 25:8 say the purpose of a sanctuary is?

_____

_____

_____

_____

_____

In 2005, when Hurricane Katrina hit, I was living in Houston. Living in Houston meant that every summer, we had threats of hurricanes and storms, and many did materialize not only in Texas but in the neighboring states as well. But then Katrina hit! It did not matter how common storms were; this major hurricane demolished lives like nothing I had ever seen before. The scenes of people trying to get on busses that were coming to Houston from Louisiana were some of the most heart-wrenching moments. Families carrying in their hands all the belongings they could, with their children, walking for hours to get the help that would hopefully take them out of Louisiana. The coast guards having to make the tough decisions of turning people away when the busses got too full or the stadium that had been housing people filled up. *National Geographic* dubs it "the costliest storm in U.S. history, and its effects are still felt today in New Orleans and coastal Louisiana."[1]

---

1 Sarah Gibbens, "Hurricane Katrina, Explained," National Geographic Society, January 16, 2019, www.nationalgeographic.com/environment/article/hurricane-katrina.

As I learned about hurricanes that summer, news anchors reported that the eye of the storm was not only the calmest part but also the furthest to reach in a hurricane. I could not help but think that Houston, even though it was slightly hit, to those in Louisiana, probably felt so far to get to. Similarly, seeing the end of the challenges we face can often feel so farfetched—with no end in sight. You may ask, "Will I ever get there? Will I be able to make it through this storm?"

Like the people of Israel in 2 Chronicles 20:8, live in that place that brings you peace, the place that restores, the place where, when the storm is raging harder than you can contain, you can build the sanctuary for His name.

What are things you do that get you in a zone where even the storm cannot touch? Mine was the classroom and the therapy room. Teaching and having sessions gave me purpose. Can you identify what it is that you do that gets you in a zone where, for just a moment, you actually don't think about the storm? Write them down here:

_____

_____

_____

_____

_____

One thing we've learned from King Jehoshaphat thus far is that even while the armies were fast approaching, he did not just sit back. He strategized; he continued to lead his people. It is important when you are going through the storms of life not to stop and only focus on the storm but to continue with your regular schedule.

This gives you purpose, but more so, note that the enemy would want all other aspects of your life to fall off track. Don't let it happen.

For example, if you have lost your job, keep applying for others or find small ways to make money through sales of your personal merchandise even as you mend the hurt of that job loss.

As we conclude, commit these things you have listed to prayer that God gives you the paradigm shift of continuing to keep your regular schedule to help you find other ways to make ends meet while you wait for that new and better job. As for the family members, support your loved ones in strategizing different ways to make some money, offer some ideas that could help. Whereas the job loss is an individual loss, the pain is one the family bears.

List five things you are most grateful for today.

_____

_____

_____

_____

_____

THE PANIC BUTTON

One night, I was sitting, having dinner; no one else was home. It was one of those nights when everyone was having a late night. I had come home from a long day, taken a shower, and got into my pajamas. Now, suppose you are like me: once the pajamas are on, that means I'm in for the night. It's about relaxing and winding down.

Just as I was eating, I got an alert on my phone, saying that my brother was in trouble, and it showed the location where he was. I *panicked*! I would want to tell you that I maintained calm, was levelheaded, and knew exactly what to do. No, I was all in this panic, like, well immersed: heart palpitations, racing thoughts, you name it. I was right there, smack-dab in a panic. Can I just pause here and say: with all the action movies I watch, one would think I would have sprung into action. Remember: I was in my pajamas; there was no time to change. I do remember looking again at the map as I strategized how I would get to him. I noticed that it was very close to my office. This was the first time it had ever happened. I didn't even know how that message came to me. Anyway, what mattered: the message was there, and I needed to get to him as quickly as I could. My plan was to grab my bag and keys and, in my pajamas, get as fast as I could to where he was. Let's take another pause; let me explain what I mean: by "pajamas," I mean pajamas, the fluffy lavender nightgown, a pink bonnet, and flip-flops—get the picture—and food in my mouth, to top it off.

All the while, I had no strategy for what I would do once I got there. Like, if it's a carjacking situation, do I follow the car? My mind was racing with all sorts of scenarios, which, I must say, is a really bad idea when you are trying to maintain calm. Instinctively, I decided to call my brother, which, to this day, I'm not sure is the best idea because what if the carjackers answer the phone, then what? I really need to go for the safety classes.

So, anyway, the phone rang, and I was standing still because I was not sure what or who I'd get on the other line. Phew! My brother answered, but because everything was moving a mile a minute, I frantically asked him where he was and if he was okay. He noticed the panic in my voice, and just as I explained the message I got on my phone, he said, "Oh, no, I'm so sorry. I pressed a button on my phone that set off a panic alert to my emergency contacts." "What?" I exclaimed as my heart rate immediately dropped to a calmer rate, my hands stopped sweating, and even though I was alarmed, I was so relieved. Just as this was happening, my mother called me in a panic because she, too, had received the message and immediately asked me where my brother was. I explained to her what happened, and eventually, we laughed it off.

What we did not know was that my brother's new watch had this safety feature on it. I, actually, at some point, thought it was a prank. But the question here is: What do we do when the panic sets in? What steps does one take when a panic situation arises? Let's see what the king and his people did when the heart-clenching moment came. We see that we need strategies so as not to get caught off guard, like in my situation above.

In his communication with the Lord in 2 Chronicles 20:9, King Jehoshaphat listed potential calamities, what were they?

_____

_____

_____

_____

_____

_____

What does he say they will do?

_____

_____

_____

_____

_____

_____

What does he say God will do in response?

_____

_____

_____

_____

_____

_____

Another place where we see someone listing the calamities and asking God to hear him is in 2 Chronicles 6:28–30. When Solomon is saying his prayer of dedication, he, too, lists several calamities and asks God to hear His people from heaven, His dwelling place.

What calamities did he list?

_____

_____

_____

_____

_____

_____

_____

Each person is aware of his or her own what?

_____

_____

_____

_____

_____

_____

_____

God will:

_____

_____

_____

_____

_____

_____

Like Solomon and King Jehoshaphat, you should know what to do when calamity strikes. Who would you call, like my brother, who is on your emergency list? Make your list here and strategize what practical things you would do in an emergency.

Emergency contact:

_____
_____
_____
_____
_____
_____

Practical things you can do:

_____
_____
_____
_____
_____
_____

Packing to evacuate town when Katrina hit was one of the most compelling challenges I went through. Whereas Houston was not badly hit, there was a time when the eye shifted and looked like it was coming for Houston, so we had been advised to evacuate. My family and I drove to Dallas, but in preparing for that trip, when we only had hours to pack, I found myself making the tough decision of what to pack and what to leave, which documents must come with me, and which ones stayed. I could only take what would fit in my car. The anxiety of not knowing if I find my apartment washed over or still intact swam through my mind the whole time. But there was something about anchoring ourselves in what was true. What was true was: we had Jesus; we were safe; we were all together, and we had somewhere to go. That reassurance was what we held onto and reminded each other of.

What can you stand on this week that will give you the reassurance that all will be okay? What scriptures can you use? Write them down here:

_____

_____

_____

_____

_____

_____

To add to your list, write down Psalm 32:7 here.

_____

_____

_____

_____

_____

_____

What does it mean to you?

_____

_____

_____

_____

_____

_____

May God create a hunger in you for Him during this week that you get to see Him as your protector and that when panic grips your heart, you know to run to Him immediately.

List down the five things you are most grateful for today.

_____

_____

_____

_____

_____

_____

ARE YOU KIDDING ME?

Have you ever been in an unfair situation where you clearly were not in the wrong but had to be the "bigger person"? While I was in college, a friend wronged me. It was clear that she indeed was in the wrong. One night, while I was at a concert with some other friends of mine, I was faced with a tough decision. The food was delicious; the music was great, and we were enjoying ourselves. Lots of the college students attended this concert, including the lady who had wronged me.

During the concert intermission, I had a deep impression on my heart of God asking me to go and apologize to the lady. *Are You kidding me?* I retorted back in my head. I went on to *remind* God what this girl had done to me. You know that moment when you are trying to make a point, but the other person is looking at you, like, "I'm just going to let you finish this rant, but ultimately, you will still have to accomplish the task"? That's what I felt God was doing.

So, I knew that if I kept this to myself, I could successfully talk myself out of it. Like, did I really hear from God, or was that just my imagination? So, I decided to tell the friend I came with to the concert so she could keep me accountable. You know what else I thought was unfair? For the rest of the concert, I was stuck with this thing in my head about what I had to do, so

I did not fully enjoy the second half as I could have. Yeah, I also tried telling God that, too—a girl had to try.

Once the concert was over, I walked over to her and said I was sorry. Here's the thing about these sort of situations: not only must you say you are sorry but sound it, have a pure spirit when saying it, and be at peace. And I did; it was tough, as I truly could not see the justice in it. But God knows what He is doing when He asks you to be the "bigger person."

Similarly, in today's verse (2 Chronicles 20:10), we see the king lamenting to God by listing the peoples who have wronged Judah: the Ammonites, Moabites, and the men from Mount Seir. Before we go deeper into that verse, let's reflect on moments when we, too, felt wronged and read some scriptures of other instances where children of God are wronged.

Write down a time when you had to be the bigger person or when a situation was so unfair based on your request and what you had done for this person.

_____
_____
_____
_____
_____

We are invited to a scenario where Moses is making a request to the king of Edom, who had "not been nice" to him. Read Numbers 20:14–21.

Fill in the blanks below from verses 17–21.

"'Please_____ your
country. We will _____
_ or drink water from any well.' [...] But Edom answered: 'You
may _____ _____ _____ here; if you try,
we will march out and attack you with the sword.' The Israelites replied: 'We will go along the main road, and _____

_____
for it. We only want _____
on foot—nothing else.' Again they answered: 'You may not pass
through.' The Edom came out against them with a large and
powerful army. Since Edom_____ to
let them go through their territory, Israel _____
_____."

Isn't it interesting that no matter how many times the Israelites
tried, they still got rejected? They tried explaining how painless
the walk through their country would be, but no. The Israelites
even took responsibility ahead of time that if they or their live-
stock drank Edom's water, they would pay them back.

It sounds as if they had a reasonable request, but no, they still
did not get permission to pass through.

Let's pause for a moment and look at the words "pass through."
In times of challenges, we can often look for the easiest way
out, but there is something about "passing through," as in going through all of it, the hills and the valleys of the situation
that God uses to build character. Taking the shortcut doesn't
bear great fruit. I've heard it often said that good comes to
those who wait. Have you ever tried to take the shortcut while
going through a challenge, only to find yourself back in the very
beginning?

Share that story here and, as you listen to the other study or family members' examples, see if you can pick out some themes among all your stories.

_____
_____
_____
_____
_____
_____

Read 2 Chronicles 20:10.

As King Jehoshaphat continues to cry out to God regarding the armies coming their way, in verse 10, we see him lamenting in disbelief, "Men from Ammon, Moab, and Mount Seir, whose territory you would not allow Israel to invade when they came from Egypt; so they turned away from them and did not destroy them." He is emphasizing the unfair situation of these very same people who were in the wrong, and God asked them to let them go by turning away from them. If that was not enough, now here they are, the very same people, coming to destroy King Jehoshaphat and his people. It sounds quite unfair.

In what way did God ask King Jehoshaphat and his people to be the "bigger people" in verse 10 above?

_____
_____
_____
_____
_____
_____

In Deuteronomy 2:4–6, 9, 18–19, what instructions does God give Moses and his people?

_____

_____

_____

_____

_____

_____

What did God say He would not give them if they provoked the people (Moabites) who lived in Seir to war?

_____

_____

_____

_____

_____

_____

We learn from this passage that God expects us to carry out His precepts even when the circumstances do not appear to warrant them. But know that He is not merely being unfair but is rather using these situations to strengthen you and, in His time, will come and resolve the challenge for you. It could be this very situation you and your family are going through. So, stand firm and see the deliverance God is about to take you through.

In some situations, you might find that you did pray about it and were sure God gave you the green light to go ahead with that particular application (for example), but now you find yourself in such a stressful situation and are wondering, "But God, You told me to apply for this. Why then has my application been denied?"

Let's go to Matthew 14:22–36 and see if we can get some insight from there. Let me draw your attention to specific verses:

> Immediately Jesus made the disciples get into the boat and go on ahead of him to the other side, while he dismissed the crowd. [...] But Jesus immediately said to them: "Take courage! It is I. Don't be afraid." "Lord, if it's you," Peter replied, "tell me to come to you on the water." "Come," he said. Then Peter got out of the boat, walked on the water and came toward Jesus. But when he saw the wind, he was afraid and, beginning to sink, cried out, "Lord, save me!" Immediately Jesus reached out his hand and caught him. "You of little faith," he said, "why did you doubt?"
>
> Matthew 14:22, 27–31

In your Bible, circle the words "Jesus made" in verse 22 and write number one above it; circle "Take courage! It is I Don't' be afraid" in verse 27 and write number two above it; circle all of verse 28 and write number three above it. Then finally, circle "Lord, save me" in verse 30 and write number four above it. These are four key points that highlight Jesus's attitude toward the raging wind and how, irrespective of this, He still encourages Peter to go ahead.

In this passage, we see that Jesus indeed instructs the disciples to get into the boat. Our point number one says He made them get into the boat—not a suggestion but a command. The boat was "buffeted by the waves because the wind was against it" (Matthew 14:24).

Why would Jesus ask them to get into the boat, knowing that the strong winds would go against it?

_____

_____

_____

_____

_____

Perhaps we see the answer in our second point: "Take courage! It is I. Don't be afraid," as well as in verse 31, when He asks Peter, "Why did you doubt?"

It is not that He was setting them up to fail or be in trouble but rather to build their character and trust in *Him*. Whatever storm He may allow you to be in, *He* is faithful to bring you out of it, so have faith.

Pen down a situation or time when you knew you had prayed and sought God, and He approved or made you take a particular chance, and before you knew it, the winds came blowing.

How did that situation end up? Did you trust or doubt God?

_____

_____

_____

_____

_____

Doubting when the storms are blowing can happen to the best of us. We see it happen to Peter, one of His disciples. But instead, Jesus does not punish him but rather encourages him. He says, "Take courage!" Did you notice the exclamation mark after "courage"? That's a statement, a command, a "stand firm" message. In the same way, Jesus is saying to you, "Take courage!"

If you have doubted, like Peter, cry out to God and say, "Lord, save me!"

What do we see happen in verse 31?

_____

_____

_____

_____

_____

In your Bible, highlight the word "immediately." As the minute Peter cried out, Jesus *immediately* reached out His hand and caught him. *Wow.* Such love our Father in heaven has for us that even when He has given us instructions and we doubt Him due to our "little faith," He does not hold that against us but comes to our rescue *immediately*. Let that soak in.

As we close today's study, remember that Jesus is saying to you, "Why did you doubt?" He wants you to have faith in Him and know that He has you. Do not be afraid.

What are you most grateful for today? List five things.

_____

_____

_____

_____

_____

_____

_____

THE POWER
OF THE FAMILY

INHERITANCE

"See how they are repaying us by coming to drive us out of the possession you gave us as an inheritance"

2 Chronicles 20:11

According to the *Merriam-Webster Dictionary*, "inheritance" by definition is "the acquisition of a possession, condition, or trait from past generations."[2] So, by this definition, inheritance is top-down, passed on from one generation to the next, which means that it is vertical and can never be horizontal. In 2 Chronicles 20:11, King Jehoshaphat highlights that the enemies were actually trying to drive them out of their land (inheritance) that had been given to him and his people by God.

Anyone who comes to try and steal another's inheritance we see, by definition, is out of line, as inheritance is passed on like a baton in a relay race: from one person directly to the next.

Unfortunately, in the present day, we still see this happening when cases of families fighting for the inheritance that has been stolen from them, and by others close to them, no less, inundate the court systems. During these storms, you may find that which was rightfully yours is being taken away. But as we will see later in today's study, God fights for you to get back what was stolen.

2 *Merriam-Webster Dictionary*, s.v. "inheritance," accessed March 20, 2022, www.merriam-webster.com/dictionary/inheritance.

How do we know this? Read Joel 2:25–27 and share with your family what these three verses highlight for you, specifically in regard to things you have lost.

You can write them here:

_____

_____

_____

_____

_____

We also see Asaph in Psalm 83:1–12, making a plea to God along the same vein as King Jehoshaphat. He is asking God to help him, for the war is threatening.

As you read this psalm, be comforted in knowing that many who have gone before us were faced with similar challenges, and the thing they had in common was that they all sought after God to rescue them.

Isn't it encouraging to know that God is still the same today and that we can cry out to Him for His protection as we are dealing with our own armies? That we, too, can pray, saying, "O God, do not keep silent; be not quiet, O God, be not still" (Psalm 83:1).

I have found that writing verses down helps remember them better. Write down today's verse, 2 Chronicles 20:11, here:

_____

_____

_____

_____

_____

What inheritance would you say that God has given you for your possession? List all of it here.

_____

_____

_____

_____

_____

Which of those have been threatened to be taken away? These may also be in relation to your personality, character, gifts, and talents. For example, the fruits of the Holy Spirit are our inheritance from God. Perhaps your joy has been taken away by the enemy, or your peace.

In what ways can you get your possessions back? What specific things can you do this week that (start to) get it or them back?

_____

_____

_____

_____

Here's a different thought: I have found that sometimes, we, too, can be our worst enemies. That, with all the inheritance that God has given us, we can sometimes sabotage our own blessings. Is this true for you? If so, in what ways do you sabotage yourself?

_____

_____

_____

_____

If this is true or not true for you, the good news is that we seek help from the same God. So, perhaps your prayer today, as we conclude, is that God helps you fight off the enemy that is trying to steal your inheritance, that He may help you stop sabotaging your inheritance. Either way, go to Him today and see Him start to fight for you.

What five things are you most grateful for today? List them here.

_____

_____

_____

_____

_____

_____

HELP

In today's study, we look at 2 Chronicles 20:12. As 2 Chronicles 20 has been the anchor chapter for this Bible study, each week, we have slowly been going through this story verse by verse. This record of King Jehoshaphat is demonstrative of the power of the family, what to do when the armies of life come at us, and what we do once the victory is won. Today we get a bit vulnerable because we learn from King Jehoshaphat about the importance of asking for help.

This story is my favorite story in the Bible; it is so layered with gifts that even if you took out just one verse, you could run with it and slay giants. I guess that's true for the entire Bible. I must say, though, I am so excited for you, knowing that you get to learn these crucial fighting strategies, that you have a Father in heaven who is your first responder. He is going to fight this battle for you, and He shows you exactly how to win. Furthermore, He ensures that what was lost is repaid and you are never "shamed" again, as we read yesterday.

I am humbled to think that my story is being used to bless you and encourage you. He thought about you who is doing this Bible study; He knew that you would need this guide to help you navigate this challenge before you; He wrote this for you—what a precious God He is!

Well, let's continue. So, today, let's learn about asking for help.

When the storms blew harder for my family, we got to a place where, as a family, we had to ask for help. On a personal level, asking for help has never been an issue, for, in my career, the great aspect is about helping people, so I know the importance of it. However, I also know that asking for help is something many people struggle with. I often hear people say, "I do not want to burden people. What will they think about me?" Others say, "People usually come to me for help, so I do not want them to think I am weak."

So, let's start there: asking for help is actually a strength. It takes a lot of courage to ask for help, and as humans, we need each other. When you are going through stuff as a family, many cultures have it that you do not speak to others about the family challenges. You do not air out your dirty laundry. But maybe the problem is not asking for help in itself but rather the definition we hold to be true. Whereas we do need to protect the family and not flippantly tell all the family business to others, there is a difference when you are in crisis and need help. Might I add here? It's been amazing to see the positive shift more people are taking toward seeking mental health services. As a therapist, I'm always so encouraged by the client who comes in and says they struggle, asking for help, but want to be better at it. There is such courage in being able to identify an area of one's life that needs some personal growth.

What does asking for help mean to you?

_____

_____

_____

_____

_____

How did you get to that definition?

_____

_____

_____

_____

What does asking for help mean for your family?

_____

_____

_____

_____

_____

Read Joshua 1:1–9. Write down each verse below:

Verse 1

_____

_____

_____

Verse 2

_____

_____

_____

Verse 3

_____

_____

_____

Verse 4

_____

_____

_____

Verse 5

_____

_____

_____

Verse 6

_____

_____

_____

Verse 7

_____

_____

_____

Verse 8

_____

_____

_____

Verse 9

_____

_____

_____

The title of this chapter is "The Lord *Commands* Joshua." This day, God is commanding you, as He did Joshua, to be strong and courageous (verse 6). Ask for the help you need. Don't let the negative thoughts talk you out of being vulnerable. In what areas do you need help? List them here:

_____
_____
_____
_____
_____

I can only imagine what it was like facing the Jordan river as the children of Israel, and the only thing they had was God's Word. As in, "the only thing they had was God's Word." Not as a deficit but as an all-encompassing fact! That is *all* they needed.

What does God say to Joshua in verse 9? Rewrite it again here and insert your name where appropriate in the verse.

_____
_____
_____
_____
_____

How else would they have been able to cross the Jordan river?

_____
_____
_____
_____
_____

We see in Joshua 3:15 that the river was at the "flood stage all during harvest," meaning it was overflowing from upstream. No one else would have been able to part it. Ask Him for help for the situation you are facing that *no one* else can solve.

As you prepare to go into that job interview, ask God for help.

As you go to see the doctor, ask God to intervene on your behalf.

As you deal with that child who seems to have fallen astray, ask God for help.

Now, this is where it gets more vulnerable: In whichever circumstance you are in, who around you—your friends or family—can you ask for help from? Write down their name(s).

_____
_____
_____
_____
_____
_____

Let's pause and pray for God to give you strength and courage as He did Joshua, that you are able to face the situation before you. Ask someone in the group to pray for all of you. If you are doing this study for yourself, take a moment to pray the same.

Here are some verses to encourage you as you wait for God's help.

In 2 Chronicles 20:12, the king is crying out to God, reiterating that they have no power to face the vast army that is attacking them. "We do not know what to do, but our eyes are upon you," he says.

In Judges 11:27, Jephthah sent the king of Ammon a message. He says, "I have not wronged you, but you are doing me wrong by waging war against me. Let the LORD, the Judge, decide the dispute this day between the Israelites and the Ammonites."

Psalm 25:15 says, "My eyes are ever on the Lord, for only he will release my feet from the snare." As you ask for help, even though it is from a fellow human being, keep your eyes fixed on Jesus.

"Turn to me and be saved, all you ends of the earth; for I am God and there is no other" (Isaiah 45:22).

"But as for me, I watch in hope for the LORD, I wait for God my savior; my God will hear me" (Micah 7:7).

God has heard your prayer. He has seen your tears. He hears the sigh when words fail; wait and see the deliverance of the Lord. He does not turn a deaf ear to His children. He sees your eyes focused upon Him. So, what do you do at the moment while you are waiting for His help? We get our answer from Joshua 1:7–8. What does Jesus say to Joshua that he and his people should do?

_____

_____

_____

Then, once you have done these things, what does God say will happen?

_____

_____

_____

Stand on this promise.

Second Chronicles 20:12 is the end of King Jehoshaphat's prayer. He ends his prayer with a plea for help from God. Remember the names of friends you wrote down earlier in today's study, contact them this week, and ask them to pray with you as you wait for God to help you. Remember: as King Jehoshaphat made his prayer, he was in the assembly of Judah and Jerusalem together with his people. We learned in week one that there is power in numbers. So, come together with your family and friends and seek Him.

By obeying His words, we get the reward we see in Leviticus 26:5–8. Read this verse out loud. In it, not only do we see the power that comes with obeying God but the same when we work in numbers.

As we close today's study, thank God for the family member(s) and friend(s) you can call on, and if you don't have one, pray and ask God to give you a true friend who you can stand with and that they can do the same for you. Ask Him to make it clear to you whom you can trust in this journey.

List down five things you are most grateful for today:

_____

_____

_____

_____

_____

A FAMILY THAT STANDS TOGETHER

It's the family that's there at every moment of life, during the highs and lows, the happy moments and the tough moments; the family are the ones who tend to be in all these situations. I have heard it said that a family that prays together stays together. It is my personal belief that the family is the most important unit here on the earth hence why the enemy is constantly trying to destroy families. It's the single unit that is constantly under such intense attacks. My other belief about families is that if you heal a family, you heal a nation. So, no wonder the enemy is constantly trying to destroy families: a strong united family is a strong united nation. When a family stands together, that is power, and the enemy does not like that. A strong and happy family in Christ means cohesion, success, and wholesome lives being experienced by the members. Success in their finances, success in their relationships, and ultimately, success in their relationship with God, which means the enemy cannot penetrate.

So, a strong and happy family may not be your experience. I am not blinded to the fact that you may be reading this, and your family is not close or happy, and relationships could be strained, or there could be some dysfunction. Do not be discouraged. This doesn't mean that you will not make it through the situation. Families come in various forms of relationships: your friends could be your family; your church family, too, would be a great support to you. Look beyond perhaps what may be a challenge when it comes to biological families and find other supportive relationships that can stand with you. Also, as we have seen thus far, there is power in prayer. Pray that God may restore your family. Nothing and no dysfunctional relationships are too hard for God to repair and restore.

Today we move on to 2 Chronicles 20:13. Let's see what we can glean from the king and his people regarding family.

2 Chronicles 20:13

At this point in the chapter, King Jehoshaphat has finished his prayer, and it's interesting that it doesn't say "the people" as it did earlier. In verse 13, he places emphasis on who exactly was standing there. It reads, "All the men of Judah, with their wives and children and little ones." He is making a point here: it was the family that stood there before the Lord with him. I am a firm believer that the family is the training ground for life. What a great lesson this was for the children and the little ones! Because of this demonstration by King Jehoshaphat, they grew up knowing about standing together with families in all circumstances.

When a family stands together!

We see this emphasis placed on the family in several stories in the Bible. The one I want us to focus on is the story of Paul and Silas in prison. Read Acts 16:16–40.

Paul and Silas were wrongfully prisoned. While they were in prison, an earthquake shook the foundations of the building, and the doors opened. Fearful of getting into trouble, the jailer who had been left in charge of them draws a sword to himself. Paul shouts, "Don't harm yourself! We are all here!" (Acts 16:28).

What happens next is what I want to draw your attention to. Write down verses 31–33 here:

_____

_____

_____

_____

_____

_____

_____

_____

_____

_____

_____

_____

_____

Once again, we see the emphasis on the whole family in a united front. Verse 34 goes on to say that the jailer was filled with joy because he had come to believe in God—he and his whole family.

There is power in this unit called the family. Whereas I know that not all families are cohesive or in accord, it is imperative to see that strength is drawn when a family stands together.

Was there a time when you had a situation and your family stood together? How did that pan out? Share that situation here:

_____

_____

_____

_____

_____

The word "stand" is such a powerful action and gesture: What does the word mean to you?

_____

_____

_____

_____

_____

In what ways can you and your family "stand" this week? Write down which specific situation you want to stand on.

_____

_____

_____

_____

_____

Notice that the standing came after they had prayed and sought God for help. Ephesians 6:13 says, "Therefore put on the full armor of God, so that when the day of evil comes, you may be able to stand your ground, and after you have done everything, *to stand*." Remember, in 2 Chronicles 20:4, it says, "The people of Judah came together to seek help from the LORD."

Circle "after you have done everything, to stand" in the verse above. In the same way, in 2 Chronicles 20:13, the family came and stood before God after the prayers were done, after they had done all they could.

So, let's ensure you have done all you can.

Have you prayed and worshiped over this situation with your family? If not, perhaps you can start with this prayer:

> *Dear Jesus,*
> *We come before You with thanksgiving in our hearts that even as we are dealing with this challenge, You are still seated on the throne and that this situation has not caught You by surprise. We thank You for our family and pray that You forgive us for any wrongs we have done, for anything we have done that has not been pleasing in Your sight. We pray that You step in where past hurts and dysfunction have torn us apart, that You unite us, Father, so that we can strengthen our resolve and learn to stand together in the power of this family unit. And we pray that You go before us in this situation and protect us from these armies coming toward us, Father, that You fight this battle for us, that You protect us as we go through this situation. We claim, Father, that nothing formed against us shall prosper. In Jesus's name, we pray, amen.*

In conclusion: standing means that you continue to pray and meditate on His Word.

What five things are you most grateful for today?

_____

_____

_____

_____

_____

THE MESSENGER

Whether individually or as a team/family, when you are standing in prayer through some things, God will always give you an answer. If you are praying with others, then it is not unlikely for Him to speak to one of the people you are standing with during this time. Or He can also use someone completely different and out of your circle to speak to you.

We are now in 2 Chronicles 20:14, where one of the people standing in the assembly, keeping their eyes on Jesus for help, gets a message from God to give to King Jehoshaphat and his people. There is something special about being a messenger: the person whose message you are delivering trusts you with that message. You have a delicate expectation to deliver as received.

Not too long ago, I purchased a gift for my brother online. The store clerk said that they indeed delivered, so once I would be ready to pay and let them, they would organize the delivery. So, I saw the pictures of the gift I had chosen and made my purchase. In a couple of hours, the gift arrived, but the package was torn and tampered with. It looked as if they sent me the window-display item box. The item on the inside looked okay, but if the box was tampered with, there was no telling about the condition of the actual merchandise. I called back, and the store clerk was quick to blame the delivery rider. I knew it could not have been the rider, as the rip on the box was an old tear. But the clerk was adamant that the messenger was at fault. Needless to say, I returned the gift and had them deliver a different one, this time, making sure that what was being brought was, in fact, what I selected and confirmed. The messenger ensured that what I ordered was what he delivered.

Let's start by reading 2 Chronicles 20:14: "Then the Spirit of the Lord came on Jahaziel son of Zechariah, the son on Benaiah, the son of Jeiel, the son of Mattaniah, a Levite and descendant of Asaph, as he stood in the assembly."

Have you ever received a message from God from one of His children or someone He uses? If so, who was it?

_____

_____

_____

_____

_____

I think about being in a restaurant and the waiter coming to notify you that your food, which has indeed taken longer than it should have, is on its way. In the waiting time, you may find it a bit anxiety provoking, not knowing what could be going on with your order. But even if it takes a bit longer, there is something about having the waiter give you an update on the progress. It settles your heart.

Here is another point to consider: the message from God came to Jahaziel "as he stood in the assembly." Standing, as we learned yesterday, is a crucial posture to take when facing an army. Standing means you continue to pray, stand on His Word, worship Him regardless of how the circumstances look.

So, as you wait for a messenger of the Lord to bring you the message of or for God Himself to speak to you, *stand*.

Read 1 Chronicles 12:18. We see warriors, as the title states, joining David. It was during this time that David got to see who was on his side and who he had to go through this war with. Similarly, when you go through tough times is when you get to know who your friends are. Often this is deemed a painful process when you discover that the persons you thought were with you are actually not; it may be painful for a little while, but it is refreshing to know who really is standing with you. Perhaps we spend so much time ruminating about the betrayal that we lose time to celebrate those who are actually with us.

Who would you list down as your Jahaziel, the person(s) who stood there with you as you all waited for God's deliverance? Write their names here.

_____

_____

_____

_____

_____

These are people you can count on who have weathered the storm or two with you. This week, let them know how grateful you are for their having been by your side. What specific things will you thank them for?

_____

_____

_____

_____

_____

I wonder: On the flip side, would your name appear on their list? Have you stood with them or other friends in the same way? We must not be quick to want loyal friends if we ourselves are not willing to *be* loyal friends. What can you do during this time to lend yourself to a friend? Write it here.

_____

_____

_____

_____

_____

There is something about helping others or volunteering or giving of your services when you are going through a storm. It gives you a sense of encouragement: you know that even in your darkest times, you were still able to help someone else.

As we close, take time to pray for those who have been standing with you during this period. Ask God to bless them a hundredfold and cover them in all of their ways. If there is anything specific you know that they, too, are believing for, use this time to intercede for them.

What five things are you most grateful for today?

_____

_____

_____

_____

_____

THE BATTLE IS NOT YOURS!

To be honest with you, I could not wait for us to get to this verse in the chapter. This is 2 Chronicles 20:15. So, yesterday, we learned that Jahaziel, while standing in the assembly, was given a message by God to give to King Jehoshaphat and his people. Just when you think that you are alone in this battle and that you will have to face this mountain alone, Jesus comes and says the most profound thing.

Write down what the Lord says to King Jehoshaphat and all who lived in Judah and Jerusalem in verse 15.

_____

_____

_____

_____

_____

This battle is *not* yours but God's. How precious is this God that He will not let your family fight the armies you are facing alone but will take them on Himself on your behalf! In 2 Chronicles 32, we see a similar situation where Hezekiah had done so much and served faithfully, only for King Sennacherib of Assyria to come and invade Judah. Let's fill in the blanks to highlight key points in this story.

Verses 7–8: "'Be strong and courageous. Do not be afraid or discouraged because of the king of Assyria and the vast army with him, for there is a _____

_____ than with him. With him is only the army of flesh, but with us is the LORD our God to help us and to _____.' And the people _____

_____ from what Hezekiah the king of Judah said."

You know, sometimes, standing on God's Word can be seen as the wrong thing to do by others or bring about doubt from those who do not believe in Jesus. You may be the laughing-stock to others and look silly to them, for the situation in the natural looks impossible, and according to them, there's no way you are going to get out of this. But in the spiritual, oh, stand firm, for God works in the supernatural! We see this in King Sennacherib's retort back to the people of Judah. In verse 10, he says, "On what are you _____

_____, that you remain in Jerusalem under siege?"

It is worth noting that our timings are not God's timings. He may not come when we want Him to, but *He* is always on time. So, the threat to give up or take a shortcut is very real, and you, too, may, at a point of weakness, see no logic in the challenge you face and ask just as King Sennacherib did in 2 Chronicles 32:10 above. *But stand*, do not give up or give in. As he asks, "Who do you base your confidence in?" reply, "Jesus." Stay the course and do not take the shortcut.

In Genesis 17, God makes a covenant with Abram, and in the covenant, several things take place. Abram's name changes to

Abraham, and in verse 15, God also says to Abraham, "As for Sarai your wife, you are no longer to call her Sarai; her name will be Sarah." Verse 16 reads, "I will _____ _____."

Read Genesis 15. We see God making a promise to Abraham about an heir. In verse 17, we see Sarah and Abraham giving in to the doubt that God would still fulfill His promise after so much time has passed. What does Sarah, in Genesis 16:1–2, suggest to Abraham that he does as a way of solving the situation?

_____
_____
_____
_____
_____

In Genesis 16:3–4, what does Abraham do?

_____
_____
_____
_____
_____

Even the best of us can tire, doubt, and fall into the trap of the enemy and take the shortcut.

What did God promise to bless Sarah with by Abraham? A _____. Then in Genesis 17:17, we read, "Abraham fell facedown; he_____ and said to himself, '_____ _____? Will Sarah _____?'"

But as we see in verse 17, God is merciful: even after Abraham had strayed, God still affirmed that the son whom He had promised would still bless both him and Sarah.

In Genesis 18, we see Sarah doubting the possibility of the promise still coming. What did Sarah do in Genesis 18:12?

_____

_____

_____

_____

_____

Fast-forward to Genesis 21: we see God's mercy at work again. Write down verse 1 of this chapter below.

_____

_____

_____

_____

_____

The Lord was gracious to Sarah and Abraham. How old was Abraham when Isaac was born (Genesis 21:5)?

_____

_____

You may look at your situation and think that God is taking too long or that He has forgotten about you. No, *He* is right on time. Tomorrow we will see how and what God wants us to do while we wait for Him to fight the battle.

The famous story of David and Goliath is one that, to this day, demonstrates God's power profoundly and how God fights for His children. Write down 1 Samuel 17:47 below.

_____

_____

_____

_____

_____

We may have a thought about how to deal with the challenges of life, but God, as is shown in 1 Samuel 17:47, highlights that His ways are not our ways. We may think that we need to fight by "sword and spear," but no, He has His ways, so stand back and watch Him fight for you. Read the following verses for yourself: Psalm 91:7–8.

I feel like adding to this: grab some popcorn and see with your own eyes how the enemy will be defeated.

On a Post-it Note, on your phone, or just someplace where you can see this reminder, write down the words, inserting your name:

_____, *the battle is not yours but the Lord's!*

(Your name here)

Another command we see in 2 Chronicles 20:15 is the Lord says, "Do not be afraid or discouraged." The challenge you are facing may be crippling you with fear or discouragement. You may have been trying out various business ventures but keep coming up short. You are tempted to give up, take an easier way out, or perhaps, you find that you are getting involved in drugs, alcohol, etc. We see the same command in Joshua 1:9. It reads, "Have I not commanded you?" This is a reminder of the command; He continues to say, "Be strong and courageous. Do not be terrified; do not be discouraged, for the LORD your God will be with you wherever you go."

Friend, why would God, in varying situations, keep telling His children to hold on and not be afraid? For us to be encouraged. Why does He repeatedly take on His children's battles and keep asking us to trust Him? Because He cares and loves us; He cares and loves your family. Also, remember it's because we see that trials have been a part of life from the beginning.

In James 1:1–6, God lets us know that, indeed, we will have trials, but our hope is in Him, for we shall not go through them alone.

Write down James 1:12.

_____

_____

_____

Let us stay encouraged, for very soon, the battle will be over. As we conclude this week, pray that God gives you the strength to continue standing and that no doubt clouds your vision as you wait. Rejoice in the fact that God has got you!

What five things are you most grateful for today?

_____

_____

_____

_____

MARCHING ORDERS

REASSURANCE

There was a time at work when we received an email stating that seventy positions were going to be made redundant due to financial challenges the company was going through. This was during the COVID-19 pandemic when businesses globally were struggling to stay afloat. This email brought on a lot of anxiety, for no one knew who the seventy were. The meeting with the president did not make things easier, as they still did not tell us whose these seventy positions were. The process of deciding was going to take a month. We all speculated and had talks amongst ourselves and even, to ease the tension, cracked jokes around the situation. Our heads of departments did not know either, but we all understood that in the next month, the company would be carrying out a series of meetings and writing letters given the process as it unfolded. In the meeting with the president, however, he mentioned that our small department was going to be tasked with providing support to those who would have to be let go. There was something about those words that gave us reassurance that perhaps we would not lose our jobs, given the work the company was setting out for us. We still did not know who the seventy were or if we ourselves would, in fact, be among them, but we held onto this reassurance, for that was all we had to go by.

In 2 Chronicles 20:16, God starts to give instructions to King Jehoshaphat. In your Bible, circle the first word of that verse, "tomorrow." This word alone could preach. When Jesus says, "Tomorrow," this gives us hope. "Tomorrow" also means that this situation will, indeed, come to an end.

You may have lost your job, but Jesus says, "Tomorrow."

The doctor's report may say one thing, but Jesus says, "Tomorrow."

Your family is struggling, but Jesus says, "Tomorrow."

Your child may be acting up, but Jesus says, "Tomorrow."

Your marriage is disrupted, but Jesus says, "Tomorrow."

Your friendships may be falling apart, but Jesus says, "Tomorrow."

Whatever the situation is, Jesus is saying to you today, "Tomorrow!"

Have hope that *tomorrow* is coming, and with tomorrow come instructions of what He wants you to do.

Let's read today's verse in King Jehoshaphat's story, 2 Chronicles 20:16.

"March down against them," Jesus says. Wait, *what*? Yesterday, God commanded the people to be courageous because running away or hiding away or putting aside the issue will not resolve it. Today, He continues to instruct them and says to march, and not just march but to do so toward the armies.

If you ever watch the soldiers marching or the marching marines, you will notice that their posture is astute, straight, confident, with precision and extreme focus. They do not move their eyes off the mark. They only listen to the soldier in command as he gives instructions.

So, as you apply for that job, go for more tests, and work on uniting your family, do so with the confidence and focus of a marching soldier.

The last sentence of verse 16 becomes very interesting: God says, "They will be _____ _____ and you will find them _____ _____." God is giving the king and his people clear instructions on where the enemies will be and at what stage of their climb. God is giving them the exact location where the enemy is, wow! Tactics in war are often said to be critically important so as to gain mileage on your opponent. Getting to know the enemy's tactic is half the battle won, for you have the ability to beat them to their own plan. And we see this happening in this verse. God is actually giving the Israelites the details on where to find the opposing armies. Without the king having this information, I would imagine, the armies would have snuck up on him and his people and taken them out. But tomorrow!

Take a moment to pray and ask God to give you direction regarding your situation. Be specific in your prayers: for example, ask whom you should speak to, where you should send your job application, which school to apply to; ask how He wants you to address your family member or coworker. Basically, what direction is God asking you to take?

You may need to come back to this section later, but if you already know, go ahead and write it now. What direction do you feel God is asking you to take?

_____

_____

_____

_____

What is (if at all) holding you back from moving in that very direction?

_____

_____

_____

_____

The Oxford dictionary states that reassurance is the action or a statement that removes someone's doubts or fears.[3] What fears or doubts do you have about marching toward your enemy's location?

_____

_____

_____

_____

Self-doubt can often be catapulted by the "what if" syndrome. This is where you talk yourself out of the situation through a series of what-ifs: "What if I'm the only one there?" "What if the results are not fruitful?" "What if I don't get the job after all I have applied to?" "What if I don't make it into that program?"

---

3 *Lexico*, s.v. "reassurance," accessed March 20, 2022, www.lexico.com/definition/reassurance.

Yeah, but what if you *do*? What's different this time is that God is right there with you.

What scriptures can you stand on to give you reassurance as you "march" toward the armies before you? Write them down here and perhaps use them as your memory verses for this portion of the battle.

_____
_____
_____
_____

Remember: your job is simply to show up but to do so in faith. God has promised that the battle, the actual fight, is not yours but His. Do your part and let Him do the impossible.

As we close today's study, rest in the reassurance that God has gone before you, that He does not waste your pain but uses it to bless you and create a testimony, that this battle you are fighting is not in vain but will reap a great harvest. Know that God has chosen you to carry His victory—what an honor! Through your story, others will come to know how mighty, undefeated, majestic, and loving our God is. Be encouraged. You are where He needs you to be.

There's a lot to be grateful for. What five things are you most grateful for today?

_____
_____
_____
_____
_____

GOD'S GOT YOU!

Learning to be still is something that did not come easy for me. But the more I've been still, the more I have seen God take care of so many a situation for me. This is not to say I get it right all the time, but I certainly have enough testimonies on the power of being still to encourage myself.

He has never lost a battle, and yours will not be the first. Let that sink in. When it came time for Moses and the Israelites to cross the sea, they made it through such a tough time. In Exodus 14:13–14, when the people doubted what God was doing, Moses reminded them,

> Do not be afraid. Stand firm and you will see the deliverance the LORD will bring you today. The Egyptians you see today you will never see again. The LORD will fight for you; you need only to be still.

Circle the word "never."

See, the "Egyptians" you are facing, like in King Jehoshaphat's case, could be very unfair. Do not reason why you have to face them. Know that suffering is part of the human experience but what is different for the children of God is that there is hope. The hope that Jesus came so that we would have life in Him.

The hope that Jesus is there to carry and walk with us through these challenges.

Suffering

Well, we all must go through suffering, as we have seen in the various stories we have read in the past weeks. But as Christians, we have hope that suffering is not in vain. Whereas it is difficult to have to face some of the painful situations we all go through, knowing that God has a track record of using that pain and turning it for good is encouraging. Genesis 50:20 says, "You intended to harm me, but God intended it for good to accomplish what is now being done, the saving of many lives." Psalm 30:5 (KJV) reminds us that "[...] weeping may endure for a night, but joy cometh in the morning."

Earlier, we saw that in Exodus 14:13–14, Moses spoke of Egyptians in the plural. Isn't it funny how problems come in multiples? It's as if they call on each other like they are going to party, "Hey, come over. Let's all bombard this person/family." I know my family has felt this way from time to time when we have been faced with varying challenges. But no matter how many they are, "The LORD will fight for you; you need only to be still." Your God has won it all.

What does "be still" mean to you? Write it down here:

_____

_____

_____

_____

We are now in 2 Chronicles 20:17, and God continues to give the instructions on what the king must do. First thing, He sets the record straight, "You will not have to fight this battle." Write down how you have anticipated fighting or in what ways you have tried to fight this challenge your way:

_____

_____

_____

_____

Isn't it refreshing to know that, well, for one, you actually don't have what it takes to fight this battle, but He who can is right there with you? You see, King Jehoshaphat and his people had probably been thinking about what weapons they could use, what armor from their stock they would carry to this war. But Jesus came and said, "Let Me deal with the impossible situation for you, My child. What I need you to do, however, is 'take up your positions': stand firm and see what God is about to do."

Why does God, at this juncture, once again remind them not to be afraid or discouraged?

_____

_____

_____

_____

What does this reminder do for you personally?

_____

_____

_____

Get out and "face" them tomorrow. There is something very deliberate and intentional about facing someone or a situation.

It's a head-on "eye to eye." So, it's one thing to go out but another to go out with one clear focus: to face the situation. Can you jot down a time when you faced a situation and how God showed up for you?

_____

_____

_____

_____

Have you ever faced a situation where you did not involve God and He had not given the direction? What was that like in comparison to the situation above (when God was involved)?

_____

_____

_____

_____

There is such comfort in knowing that the Lord is with you. Yes, this suffering has not been easy; it has caused you much pain and probably some sleepless nights. But know this: He who created the world, He who knows the number of hairs on your head, the one who sprang the stars into the sky, the one who positions the sun and the moon, the one who makes the waters rage at His command—that God is with you.

Write down Proverbs 18:24.

_____

_____

_____

_____

_____

This verse says that there is one who sticks closer than
_____. That *one* is Jesus.

God has got you: trust Him!

In closing, take a moment to pray this prayer:

> *Dear Jesus,*
> *Thank You for being there in the darkest of times. Thank*
> *You for holding us in the palm of Your hand. Thank You for*
> *sticking closer to us than a brother would. We pray that,*
> *as we go out tomorrow and face the armies in our lives, we*
> *choose to trust You and not be discouraged by the situation*
> *before us. We ask all this in Your name, amen.*

What five things are you most grateful for today?

_____

_____

_____

_____

_____

GET ON YOUR KNEES

As a child, I often saw my grandmother get on her knees while she prayed. Whereas she prayed often, it was not always that she took to her knees. For example, when she prayed for food, she never knelt down, or while sometimes praying for the family, she did not kneel down. So, the posture in prayers varied depending on the circumstance.

As a child, I never understood it, but this is what I did notice about the times she prayed while on her knees: there was a change in countenance when she was on her knees. There was humility in that posture that appeared to deepen her prayer. Other times, like in church, she lifted her hands during praise and worship. This was yet another posture that was not always done but was frequent. It was as though she was surrendering herself to God, giving Him permission to have His way in the situation. It was as though she was in reverence toward Him, which is exactly what it was. As I grew up, I learned what it meant to kneel down in prayer or to lift your hands in praise. I probably imitated her as a child, not knowing what I was doing but copying what she was doing. It was a position of reverence and surrender to the Father; it was a position of worship.

Yesterday, we learned that there was a posture God wanted us to take. We see this in 2 Chronicles 20:18.

What does it say that the people of Judah and Jerusalem did?

_____

_____

_____

_____

_____

Ultimately, we need to take on the posture of worship. In this verse, we see that they knelt or lay down in worship. Have you been able to worship during this time when you went through a challenge?

_____

_____

_____

_____

_____

What were the benefits?

_____

_____

_____

_____

_____

In previous seasons, when I faced difficult challenges in my life, I remember thinking, *I need to praise and worship.* But to be honest with you, this was not always easy. Lifting my hands felt heavy; when I went down on my knees, all I could do was break down and sob. But here's what I learned during this time. As long as your heart is turned toward Him, He hears the longing and song in your heart that the pain has clouded. So, when words failed for me, music spoke. When I couldn't utter the words, putting on praise and worship music ministered to my spirit in ways I could not explain. Before I knew it, I was singing along. It was also in those moments that God would speak to me through the songs.

So, you may be in a situation that is very painful, and like mine, your hands feel too heavy to even lift and praise. Start with where you are. If humming a tune is all you can do, start there. Before you know it, you, like my grandmother, will be lifting up your hands in surrender and kneeling down in worship.

In 2 Chronicles 20:18, we read that the king bowed his head and that the people of Judah and Jerusalem fell down in worship. Friends, gather your family, Bible study group, friends and worship the Lord together: pull heaven down together and touch the hem of His garment. Whereas you may not be in the same location with your friends, ask them this week to stand with you in worship.

You can also take some time during this study and worship together.

How can you infuse worship in your day-to-day activities this week?

_____

_____

_____

_____

_____

What time can you set aside this week to get on your knees and worship?

_____

_____

_____

_____

We learn from 2 Chronicles 20:18 that this is a requirement from God while He is fighting the battle. This is not to say that He cannot fight without our worship, but it certainly pleases God to hear the worship of His children, especially when a war is at hand. Your worship is paramount to the battle being fought.

What other forms of worship please God?

_____

_____

_____

_____

_____

As we conclude today, pray that you can fall on your knees and worship the Lord this week, that your family and friends, wherever they are, join you in this season of worship.

What five things are you grateful for today?

_____

_____

_____

_____

_____

MAKE SOME NOISE

Yesterday, we looked at various types of worship. Today we will look at 2 Chronicles 20:19. We see that while King Jehoshaphat and the people of Judah and Jerusalem fell down in worship, some Levites stood up and praised the Lord. In primary school, the teacher would take a roll call every morning, and once she called out your name, you were to stand up and state that you were present. Standing up means that you are taking a different position. You were initially seated, but now you are changing your position to stand up. Standing up is like making a declaration that you are here.

The enemy thinks he has taken you or your loved one out? Stand up and show him that you are here! The Levites stood up and praised the Lord. They made a declaration to God, "We are here, and we are praising You." This week we have been studying the importance of staying in your lane. The Levites show us how, even though the others were seated, they were not going to conform but do what they needed to do to worship during this time.

Comparison is a very toxic choice to make, which the enemy will convince you to use. You find yourself looking at the other person and their situation and comparing yourself to them. Remember this: everyone's destiny is uniquely different, and

God made us that way. He made us unique in His image and likeness. Can you imagine that every human being is created with unique fingerprints? There's no one in the world with prints like yours. God made you different for a reason, so stand up and do not compare yourself to the other person or their situation.

I learned the hard way that I should not worry about what others will think of me because the truth is they will speak about you when you don't do anything the same as when you do something.

Read 2 Chronicles 20:19.

Specifically, with what did the Levites praise the Lord?

_____

_____

_____

_____

_____

Why did they do so with a "very loud voice"?

_____

_____

_____

_____

_____

I've often wondered why police officers shout when they are making an arrest or, when going into a room in search of suspects, they make noise. But I came to realize that they are letting the enemy know who is in charge. In the moments of challenge, the enemy tries to do three things. Turn to John 10:10 and write here what those three things are:

_____

_____

_____

_____

But in the same verse, Jesus lets us know that He _____
_____ and have_____
_____.

Isn't it interesting that during this time of challenge, the enemy is trying so hard to keep you there, seated down, consumed with fear, carried away by comparison, and dimming any semblance of the light?

What untruths has the enemy been trying to feed you with every time you try to stay in your lane or stand up?

_____

_____

_____

_____

_____

Let's memorize the following truths that you can keep with you any time the enemy tries to get you off track.

Acts 9:32–34

In this story, we see Aeneas healed from paralysis, but Peter asks him to do something immediately after that. He says to him, "Get up and take care of your mat." Put action to your faith: don't be afraid to act on your faith.

Matthew 20:30–34

There are always going to be other voices countering what God is saying, countering what you know to be true about God. The verse says "the crowd" rebuked the blind men. There were many people wanting them to remain seated and do nothing about their situation. But these two blind men knew what it meant to stay in their own lane. They knew the suffering they were going through, and they were *not* going to let those with physical sight take away what their spiritual sight was showing them. What does it say they did in verse 31?

_____

_____

_____

_____

See, you need to get louder than the naysayers because there is always going to be another voice that tries to convince you not to go after the healing you need; there's always going to be another voice that tries to convince you to give up on that dream, for too much time has elapsed; there's always going to be a contradicting voice. What did Jesus say to the blind men in Matthew 20:34?

_____

_____

_____

_____

_____

Get up! In that situation that you gave up on, get up! With that child who has been walking away from the teachings of God, get up! You have gone through a divorce and have given up on ever dating again—get up! The doctors say that there is no other way but to have that surgery—get up! In what ways have you let the other voice convince you that it is not possible?

_____

_____

_____

_____

_____

Let's look at a story where God's power is highlighted in a mighty way. Read Luke 8:40–56 and write verse 49 here:

_____

_____

_____

_____

What did the "someone" say to Jairus?

_____

_____

_____

_____

Where did this "someone" come from?

_____

_____

_____

_____

Note that those who will be talking you out of believing could come from "your house." Those close to us can also be the same ones speaking against what God plans and be the ones discouraging us from moving forward. They could be the ones discouraging us from following those dreams.

Why did he ask Jairus not to "bother the teacher anymore"?

_____
_____
_____
_____

Could it be that when the situation seems "dead," we stop praying, we stop standing, we stop worshiping? But also, could it be that God will ensure that it dies so as to prove that *only He* could perform that miracle? You are looking at your age and thinking, *There's no way I can go back to school now or have a baby at this age or form a relationship with my estranged family member.* If this is you, this verse is for you. Write down Luke 8:53–54 below:

_____
_____
_____
_____

See, the story is not over until Jesus says it's over. For all intense purposes, Jairus's daughter died, and what was Jesus doing while this was happening (verse 49)?

_____
_____
_____
_____

At what point had Jesus been notified that Jairus's daughter was dying?

Did He go over to the twelve-year-old girl immediately?

_____

_____

What did He do first?

_____

_____

_____

_____

_____

See, if there was anything for Jesus to have been concerned about, don't you think He would have rushed over there? That dream you let go of—Jesus is saying to you, *"Get up!"*

In verse 55, what happened once "her spirit" returned to her?

_____

_____

_____

_____

_____

Write down verse 50 below.

_____

_____

_____

_____

Why did Jesus say this to Jairus?

_____

_____

_____

_____

_____

"Just believe." Jesus is saying to you in this situation, no matter how grim it looks, "Just believe." What do you need to believe this week about that situation? Or, if you look back at a past situation, what did you need to believe that perhaps you did not?

_____

_____

_____

_____

_____

Let's close today's study in prayer.

> _Dear Jesus,_
> _Thank You for today's revelation. Thank You for restoring our spirits back to life. Give us the ability to stand back up again, rekindle that dream that we thought was dead. Jesus, You have shown us that the situation is not dead but only asleep, Father. Help us to silence the voices that go against Your teachings and those that try to give us doubt in this situation. We thank You for speaking to these dry bones and restoring them back to life. In Jesus's name, we pray, amen._

What five things are you most grateful for today?

_____

_____

_____

_____

_____

_____

_____

HAVE FAITH

Faith, as we know, is "being sure of what we hope for and certain of what we do not see" (Hebrews 11:1). The King James Version says, "Now faith is the substance of things hoped for, the evidence of things not seen." We have reached the part where King Jehoshaphat and his people are headed to face the army (2 Chronicles 20:20), but just as they are leaving, King Jehoshaphat says something to them.

Write what he says to them here:

_____

_____

_____

_____

_____

It's interesting that he chose to say this to them, and yet no one had verbally stated feeling otherwise. Could it be that he was speaking to their thoughts? Similarly as faith is the evidence of things not seen? I can certainly relate to this: being pumped up to stand and face the armies but deep down not having complete faith that God will indeed show up. This happens to the best of us; once you begin to march toward your army, the nerves can start to get the better of you. But isn't it so beautiful that God would know of this and see it fit to encourage us? We see the same thing in Luke 8:49–50:

"While Jesus was still speaking, someone came from the house of Jairus, the synagogue ruler. 'Your daughter is dead,' he said. 'Don't bother the teacher anymore.' Hearing this, _____

_____,

'Don't be _____.'"

Jairus had not said anything but God immediately spoke to his fears, which he had not even verbalized.

During that challenging season of my life, one of the things I had to keep doing was going for blood work to check that all required levels were leveling off. These were some of the hardest times, but I learned something during that period: that being courageous does not mean that you are void of fear. It means that despite the fear, you are still marching toward the army. As I would walk in the hallways of the hospital leading toward the lab, fear would often grip my heart. But I had to remind myself what I am reminding you now: keep marching toward that army. Keep the faith and *just believe* regardless of what the physical situation may look like. Fix your faith on Him and Him alone. He sees your nerves, and He is cheering you on. He is not disappointed but knows how tough this must be for you.

Write down Isaiah 7:9 below.

_____

_____

_____

_____

_____

What have you been putting your faith in?

_____

_____

_____

_____

Second Chronicles 20:20 says to have faith in the Lord, "and
you _____;
have faith in his prophets and you will _____
_____."

It is recorded in 2 Chronicles 20:20 that they left "early in the
morning," not in the afternoon or in the midmorning but early
in the morning. There is something divine about the early-
morning time: the sunrise, the peace before everyone and everything wakes up; there is something special about this time
of day. So, it is interesting that they left at this time. In several other places, we see God's people also set off early in the
morning.

Mark 1:35 says, "Very early while it was still dark, Jesus got up,
left the house and went off to a solitary place, where he prayed."

In Joshua 3:1, it says, "Early in the morning Joshua and all the
Israelites set out from Shittim and went to the Jordan, where
they camped before crossing over."

Record Joshua 6:15 here:

_____

_____

_____

_____

Discuss why you think early morning is so important.

_____

_____

_____

_____

Early morning gives purpose. When you wake up, it is important to pray and set the intention for the day. Put God over all things on that day.

How do you start your mornings?

_____

_____

_____

_____

We saw in Mark 1:35 that Jesus woke up very early, while it was still dark, and went off to a solitary place to pray. As you march toward your army, start off early in the morning with prayer, spending time with God before setting out of the door.

He has chosen you to carry His victory.

As we conclude today's study, commit your plans to God and purpose yourself to wake up early and start your day with God.

Read Proverbs 16:3. What plans do you need to commit to the Lord this week?

_____

_____

_____

_____

What five things are you most grateful for?

_____

_____

_____

_____

_____

_____

_____

_____

_____

_____

THE POWER OF YOUR PRAISE AND WORSHIP

THE WOW FACTOR

It is befitting that in the last week's study, we learned about the importance of having and putting our faith in God, and we begin this week at what we do even before God fights the battle for us. We are now in 2 Chronicles 20:21 and see an interesting request from King Jehoshaphat.

What does he appoint men to do?

_____

_____

_____

_____

For what purpose were they to praise the Lord?

_____

_____

_____

_____

When were they to sing?

_____

_____

_____

What position in the context of the army did they take?

_____
_____
_____
_____
_____

What did they sing?

_____
_____
_____
_____
_____

The power of praise is one that we see throughout the Bible. Praise and worship are the weapons God has given us to tackle any situation. Isn't it interesting that the king appointed praisers and worshippers? Furthermore, he strategically placed them at the head of the army. This brings to our attention that before you go and face your army, you should start praising and worshipping the Lord. Before you get that job, before the healing comes, before the family is reunited, start praising Him for what's yet to come. But their praise and worship was specific; it was thanksgiving, wow! Even before the battle is won, we should be saying thank-you to the Lord for His holiness and splendor.

For example, any time we render services at the dry cleaner's, we wait to ensure that the clothes are properly laundered before we pay and say thank-you. But because of our faith and trust in God and because of who He is, we praise *before*.

Write down the things you can start thanking God for even though they have not yet been accomplished:

_____

_____

_____

_____

Now, given the situation you are in, you may not be able to praise and worship at the same time: while taking the exam or completing an interview, or, perhaps, you are going in for a medical procedure. So, who can you appoint to praise and worship ahead of your battle?

_____

_____

_____

_____

In 1 Chronicles 16:29, we see the same concept as that of David's Psalm 29:2, where he gives his account of thanks to the Lord. First Chronicles 16:29 states, "Ascribe to the LORD glory due his name. Bring an offering and come before him; worship the LORD in the splendor of his holiness." In Psalm 29:2, it states, "Ascribe to the LORD the glory due his name; worship the LORD in the splendor of his holiness."

Write down Psalm 96:8 in the space below.

_____

_____

_____

_____

Did you notice that in these three verses, the people of God were not thanking Him for having fought the battle or having accomplished the task? They were simply thanking Him for who He is! Add to the list below, stating who God is to you:

Yes, He is mighty.
He is your champion.
He is almighty.
He is sovereign.
He is love.
He is peace.
He is your Father.

He is _____.

He is _____.

He is _____.

He is _____.

He is _____.

Read the following verses:
- Colossians 2:10
- Ephesians 2:5
- Isaiah 54:14
- 1 John 5:18
- 1 Corinthians 2:16
- Philippians 2:5
- 1 John 4:4
- Luke 6:36–38

Select from some of the scriptures above and write down who
He says you are:

_____
_____
_____
_____

Why do we need to give thanks for who He is?

_____
_____
_____
_____

God does not cease being God based on the battle. Irrespective
of the battle you are facing, *He* continues to be God. And from
Hebrews 13:8, we know that Jesus Christ _____
_____
_____
_____.

If you go back to your list of who you say God is, then just that
alone is reassurance and confidence that you have the Almighty
by your side. Rest in that.

When the ark was being brought to the temple in 2 Chronicles
5:13, the musicians took their positions and praised the Lord
Almighty. What did they sing to the Lord?

_____
_____
_____
_____

We thank You, Jesus, for teaching us the power of our praise and worship to You.

The psalmist in verse 136:1 indicates why we give thanks to the Lord. Simply: for He is good. His love endures forever!

As we conclude today's study, you should stand firm, knowing that God is God, He is merciful, He loves you, and He is by your side in every step of the challenges you face.

What five things are you most grateful for?

_____

_____

_____

_____

_____

YOU HAVE THE AUTHORITY

Several years ago, I got invited to be the guest of honor at my high school prize-giving day. The current principal had been a class teacher in several of our classes when we were in school. It had been many years since I had spoken to her, but her voice was distinct, never to be forgotten. Her voice alone commanded an audience; it was clear, precise, and sure. It had authority.

My phone rang; it was a number I did not know. "Hello!" the caller said. Would you believe I nearly stood up in my office, for it did not matter how many years it had been: I knew that voice from any other! In my speech, I started with this story, and the students and faculty alike laughed, for they knew what I was talking about. They, too, knew this distinct voice of authority.

Authority

The Oxford dictionary states that the word "authority" means "the power or right to give orders, make decisions, and enforce obedience."[4]

---

4 *Lexico*, s.v. "authority," accessed March 20, 2022, www.lexico.com/definition/authority.

God has given you authority over any and all of the enemies you may face in life. He has given you authority over that situation, over that family challenge, over your hurt, over your relationship, over the disobedience your child has chosen to live in, over your financial status. Jesus has given you authority! This is amazing news.

Remember we read John 10:10 in a previous study? This time, highlight the second part of the sentence that says why Jesus came. Write it here:

_____

_____

_____

_____

_____

Write down what Proverbs 18:21 says:

_____

_____

_____

_____

_____

The power lies in your tongue. What have you been speaking over your situation?

_____

_____

_____

_____

_____

If the above are not in alignment with what God says about your situation, list here godly truths that you can recite over your situation.

_____

_____

_____

_____

In my line of work, affirmations are part of the healthy nuggets we introduce to clients. See, you cannot show up to a marathon, not having trained, and expect to finish successfully. Months before the race, you have to train over and over again. In the same way, rehearse by reciting the above truths, repeating them at every point you get, letting the words minister and sink deep into your spirit. Before you know it, you will begin to believe these truths.

Let's see the power of praise as demonstrated in the story of King Jehoshaphat. In your Bible, highlight the first three words in 2 Chronicles 20:22. It was not after they had finished praising; it was "as they began." Do not underestimate the power in your praise!

_____

_____

_____

_____

What did God do as they began to sing and praise?

_____

_____

_____

Let's study what an ambush looks like. Read 2 Chronicles 13:13–14.

Where did Jeroboam set troops?

_____
_____
_____
_____
_____

What was his intention?

_____
_____
_____
_____
_____

God is not going to let the army you face come at you from any side. He has them surrounded from every side. Take note: He set ambushes around all camps that could have been wanting to attack King Jehoshaphat and his people. Many a time, troubles come in multiples, but this verse reassures us that regardless of how many challenges you are facing, God will set ambushes for each of them.

Highlight the last four words of verse 22 and write them down here:

_____
_____
_____
_____

Yes, they were defeated! Isn't this encouraging? The armies that were impossible to defeat for them had now been defeated. I can only imagine what joy this brought to King Jehoshaphat and his people.

How will you utilize your authority this week?

_____

_____

_____

_____

_____

As we close today, begin thanking God for the revelations He has shown you thus far through this study. Thank Him for the specific ways He has given you to conquer the enemy. Thank Him for the authority that He has given you. And ask Him to strengthen you when you are weak or overcome by doubt.

What five things are you most grateful for today?

_____

_____

_____

_____

_____

CONFUSION

We had a hockey coach in high school who was really gifted in the game. At practice, he would teach us various dribbles, scoops, flicks, emphasizing that our techniques were paramount to winning our matches. He, however, moved so fast through his opponents, leaving them confused as to what technique he had used to get past them. So, at one home game, we had practiced as we did for all matches. The time came, and the game began; once we started, I still had my sweater on, tied around my waist. I knew the coach would not have been happy with me if (1) I ran back to the bench to place it there or (2) continued playing with it on. I chose the latter; I figured running back to the bench would slow us down, and since the game had already started, I didn't have too many options.

The game was going well: it was a great one; our team was pushing out our best tactics in the hopes that we would win. You know, the kind of game where the intensity is on, the competition between the teams is on, the techniques are being applied, and every team is fighting for their goal. Then, it started raining. So, remember that sweater I had mentioned that I had around my waist? Now listen, I had not prepared for rain and my hair, well, you know...water was not going to be part of that plan. Yes, of course, we were sweating, but pouring-down rain was another level. These were the days when we all had perms, and rain and perms just did not gel. So, yup, you guessed it. I took my sweater and wrapped it around my head like a bonnet. Might I add I had the ball at this time?

So, picture this: it's raining; we are playing hockey; I have the ball, and I'm running toward the goal, all the while trying to wrap my hair. I don't think the coach even knew what to do with me. At some point, I glanced over, and the confused look on his face was one to remember. I mean, of all the plays he had taught us, this was certainly not one of them.

He waved his hands in the air to me as if to ask, "What in heaven's name are you doing?" Please remember the game is still going on! My teammates were as tickled and confused as well. See, I saw my sweater as a provision from the Lord. I mean, no one else had their sweaters. If anyone cares to know, I considered myself quite fortunate. Needless to say, I passed the ball to my teammate, finished tying my hair, and continued with the game. The laughter in the locker room was priceless. We all laughed so hard. The coach never punished me because the truth is there was no title for my type of "technical." My mother, who was standing in the bleachers, just kept cheering me on; you've gotta love Momma. She was so focused on this intense game that she literally kept her eyes on the ball. We had a good laugh about it later when I told her the story from my perspective.

This is the part in your life where you get to laugh, for what God does with the armies that were rising up against your family is literally hilarious.

Read 2 Chronicles 20:23.

Who did the men of Ammon and the men of Moab rise up against?

_____

_____

_____

_____

_____

Once they destroyed and annihilated them, what did they do next?

_____

_____

_____

_____

_____

What does the word "annihilate" mean?

_____

_____

_____

_____

_____

In a similar manner, in Judges 7:22, what happens when the three hundred trumpets sound?

_____

_____

_____

_____

_____

In 1 Samuel 14:20, we read, "Saul and all his men _____ and went _____ _____. They found the Philistines __ _____, _____ _____ with their swords."

I mean, it's one thing to be confused, but it's another to be totally confused; there's no room for recovery after total confusion. Can I just add to the list of His many accolades—God has a sense of humor!

Can you imagine what the people of God in these three accounts must have thought when they found the armies that had been so threatening to them, that had wreaked such havoc in their lives and instilled such fear, were all in total confusion to the point of killing each other? If that doesn't crack you up...

Read Ezekiel 38:21 to see yet another account where God causes confusion in the enemies' camp, destroying every one of them and saving His children. Be encouraged: this battle is not yours but the Lord's.

Read Ezekiel 39:21. In this verse, however, God talks about how He will display His glory among the nations and that "all the nations will see the punishment I inflict and the hand I lay upon them." See, God is going to make sure that the nations know that He is the one who fought for you.

Write down the last sentence of Isaiah 61:9 and insert your name where applicable.

_____

_____

_____

God has chosen His victory to shine through you. Every situation where God is involved, no matter how hard the start is, always ends in victory. What an honor!

In closing, declare Isaiah 61:7–9 over your life. Insert your name where applicable as well in all the verses.

What five things are you most grateful for today?

_____

_____

_____

_____

_____

THE EVIDENCE

Every year at work, we submit our annual evaluations. These evaluations look at various categories of expansion, and with each come varying points. However, the most important document that must accompany the checklist is our evidence. To earn the point, you must provide the evidence proving that you indeed accomplished the task or presented at the said conference or that you contributed to community service that you report to have. By the end of each year, you find that you have accumulated a lot of evidence due to all the work you have done in that year. Based on your cumulative percentage resulting from your evidence, a promotion of sorts is granted.

The flip side is true as well. Every time a storm breaks out, it leaves evidence of the damage caused: houses and trees uprooted, property thrown all over the place, and just sheer devastation. I can only imagine the sight King Jehoshaphat and his community found when all the Ammonites, Moabites, and people from Seir had been annihilated. Considering that, at some point, King Jehoshaphat was concerned about this army shows that they were well trained and perhaps had the very best of ammunition. Yet, as we read yesterday in verse 23, they rose up against each other and destroyed one another with those very well-trained skills and armor. But see: when you have the armor of God, truly, you are untouchable.

Read 2 Chronicles 20:24.

Imagine the sheer mix of emotions King Jehoshaphat and his people experienced: joy, relief, shock at the state of events, and gratitude to God for going before them. This verse says that the people came to the place that "overlooks the desert": this symbolizes that they were standing above and looking down. There is a promotion, an elevation that follows when God wins the battle for you. You do not remain the same. Nor do you remain at the same level. What an awesome truth! They *overlooked* the desert, which means that they themselves were not, or no longer, in the desert.

It is important to look back or go to that place that Jesus delivered you from to remember the miracles that He has provided for you.

List here some of the miracles you remember God taking you and/or your family through.

_____

_____

_____

_____

_____

Read Psalm 105:

Verse 1: "Give _____, call on his name; make _____ what _____."

Verse 5: "_____ he has done, _____ and the judgements he pronounced."

Verse 8: "He _____; his _____
forever, the word he commanded, for a thousand generations."

From this same Psalm 105, jot down the other promises stemming from His covenant with Abraham.

_____
_____
_____
_____
_____

It's one thing to go back to that place or remember all that God has done for you, but that is not enough: let your testimony bless someone else. See, that season of pain you went through was not only for you but for you to be a blessing to others. There could be someone else struggling with the same issues. Your struggles and triumph are meant to bring you closer to Jesus, build your faith and testimony, and help someone else. In what ways can you use your testimony to bless others?

_____
_____
_____
_____
_____

Who around you do you think needs to hear your story?

_____
_____
_____
_____
_____

Spend some time thanking God for the miracles He has given you and for those that are yet to come. At the end of each day, we have been highlighting the five things we are grateful for. What have you discovered through this exercise?

_____

_____

_____

_____

How does gratitude honor God?

_____

_____

_____

_____

_____

In Luke 17:11–17, we see the story of the ten lepers. What did the ten men in verse 13 call out to Jesus?

_____

_____

_____

_____

_____

At what point did they get healed?

_____

_____

_____

_____

_____

What did Jesus ask in verse 17?

_____

_____

_____

_____

_____

Gratitude leads to joy.

Gratitude turns the ship around from darkness to light.

It is important to give thanks to God even while the storms of life are blowing. As we close, here is your opportunity for today to give thanks to God.

What five things are you most grateful for? Remember to be specific.

Gratitude defies the enemy's lies.

_____

_____

_____

_____

_____

GIFTS IN THE STORM

When I was going through that tough season in my life, I found it very difficult to see what good would come of that. The pain blinded the vision. I knew I would get out of it because He promised that He would see me through, but what would come of it was still not clear.

When you look at the site of the hurricane, all you can see is the mess: debris everywhere, broken glass, lost possessions, just utter destruction. But once the communities begin to clean, they start to find people's fine possessions. They're gold and precious-stone jewelry, their pictures, their cherished materials, all amongst the rubble. I learned that every storm leaves gifts; the question is, will we find them?

But Jesus sees with His spiritual eyes far beyond the rubble; He sees the victory, the book you will publish, the speaking engagements you will hold, blessing others, the training you will lead, the business you will start, the organization you will run, all because of what came of that tough season in your life. He sees beyond all of it.

Write down 2 Chronicles 20:25 here:

_____

_____

_____

_____

_____

It says that there was so much plunder that it took how long to collect it?

_____

_____

_____

_____

_____

Underline "more than they could take away" in your Bible. This is so good: let's define this clearly.

The storm will leave you with more blessings than what you started with. Good God! The verse says, "There was so much plunder that it took three days to collect it." The word "collect" signifies something that is yours. You collect your package from the post office; you collect your clothes from the dry cleaner's. Prepare yourself to collect your blessings after Jesus has won the battle for you.

No matter how long it takes, be sure to collect the gifts left for you in the storm. For Jehoshaphat and his people, it took three days, which is quite a lot, considering he had a whole community working with him.

What are the gifts you have collected in the storms you have been through?

_____

_____

_____

_____

_____

How have these gifts transformed your life?

_____

_____

_____

_____

_____

How have your collected gifts blessed others?

_____

_____

_____

_____

_____

Every storm leaves gifts: the situation you went through may have been the most unfair, most painful, but even in that situation, there is a gift for you. One time, a friend asked me, "How do I ensure that I won't go through this situation again?" She happened to be going through a tough time and, in her brokenness, asked me this question. My response was, "By ensuring you have taken [learned] the gifts from that storm."

Every storm has a purpose: you may not see it at the time, but it does. For example, if you hire an employee whose character is questionable, but you keep turning a blind eye for the sake of being likable, the day they steal from the company will be a very difficult time for the organization. Now, at face value, the issue could look as if the employee who stole is the ultimate problem, but perhaps it is not. The gift in this storm is the lesson of the importance of you being authentic and not being so concerned about being likable to the point that the company is now suffering a financial loss. So, if you don't work on being authentic and being true to your values, then a similar situation will happen again. Always look deep into the storm, and as King Jehoshaphat and his men did in verse 25, go and take your plunder.

See, this bad thing happening was not so bad after all because ultimately, you gain the skill of being authentic and a better leader. Hence after a while and healing, one can look back at a storm and be grateful for it.

Read James 1:17.

What good and perfect gifts are from the Lord?

_____

_____

_____

_____

_____

It is also important to note that the gifts may be there and that we may see them, but sometimes, we ourselves can sabotage receiving them through our self-worth, self-doubt, fear, etc., doubting we deserve such a blessing. But in Ecclesiastes 5:19, Jesus reminds us,

"Moreover, when _____ gives someone _____ and _____ and _____ _____ to enjoy them, to _____ and be _____—this is a gift of God."

Remember, as is told in 2 Timothy 1:7, that "God did not give us a spirit of timidity, but a spirit of power, of love and of self-discipline."

As you complete this week's study and this verse, may God bless you.

Ephesians 3:20–21 reads, "Now to him who is able to do _____ more than all we ask or _____, according to his power that is at work within us, to him _____ in the church and in Christ Jesus throughout all generations for _____ and _____! Amen."

Let us pray:

Father, thank You for who you are. Thank You for being almighty, magnificent, all-loving and being with us in the storms of life. Help us fully accept our gifts and use them for the purposes for which You gave them to us to use. May we be a blessing to those around us. We thank You, Father. We love You. In Jesus's name, we pray. Amen.

What five things are you most grateful for?

_____

_____

_____

_____

_____

_____

_____

WEEK 6

PEACE ON
EVERY SIDE

VALLEY OF BERACAH

Throughout this study, we have been giving thanks for the simple blessings each day. How much more should we give thanks when God wins battles for us? In various cultures, it is customary to give thanks after achievements: when children do well in school, we celebrate them; when awards are won, we celebrate our loved ones. So, on a larger scale, we should not forget to come together and give thanks to God. The ultimate praise we, as believers, give God is that Jesus Christ fought the battle to save us. He paid the ultimate price, which makes us more than conquerors in Christ Jesus. He fights our battles, wins for us, and we get to share the victory: now, that's a pretty good deal, so the least we can do is praise! We praised and worshiped as we marched into the war, and we shall praise once it's over.

On the fourth day, as reported in 2 Chronicles 20:26, what did King Jehoshaphat and his people do?

_____

_____

_____

_____

_____

Did they go one by one?

_____

Where did they assemble?

_____
_____
_____

When that team of friends, family, community assembled with them to give praise to God for the miracle, how encouraged they must've felt in that moment!

Like King Jehoshaphat, gather your community in your "valley of Beracah" and have a thanksgiving service of sorts. Call on your pastor and conduct a service simply in honor of God for what He has done for you and your family. Read the following scriptures and commit one of them to memory this week as you praise God for His faithfulness:

- Ezra 3:11
- Psalm 7:17
- Psalm 35:18
- Psalm 69:30
- Daniel 2:23

Beracah means "praise."

Which one will you use as a memory verse for this week? Write it down here.

_____
_____
_____
_____

Why did the king and his people in 2 Chronicles 20:26 assemble and praise the Lord?

_____

_____

_____

_____

_____

In closing, as you prepare to have a thanksgiving service, be sure to list down the miracles, big or small, that God has provided for you during this season. Being specific as to what you are giving thanks for, I have found, serves as a great testimony to continue encouraging yourself as well as others.

What five things are you most grateful for today?

_____

_____

_____

_____

_____

_____

_____

REJOICE IN THE LORD

It was our final sports day; we were excited to be graduating from high school, and we made it known.

As most high schools do, the school was divided into four teams called "houses." I was in "green" house, and there were "red," "blue," and "yellow." Every house had its captains, cheer songs, strengths, and of course, areas of growth. So, this was it: our final year. We all had mixed emotions, profusely happy but so sad for the end of this era of our lives. Perhaps what saddened us the most was the fear of losing our friendships. I went to the same elementary, middle, and high schools, and so, if you remember, back then, our friendships ran deep. I mean, we had been together ever since the days when we used to have to pin our handkerchiefs to our collars. It was also the days when we walked with our index fingers on our lips as we got into the classroom in the morning and even had knee-high toilets and sinks because we were so small. We had been together for a long time. So, the end of this time together was hard for all of us. Yes, we had good times but also had squabbles from time to time, but all in all, those years together were going to be missed.

So, on our final sports day, I woke up in the morning, anticipating the day ahead; my mind wandered as to how this day was going to be. I had my green colors on, my autograph book because, in those days, you got all your friends and teachers to sign your autograph books. I still have mine, by the way—oh, what memories! But I was not going to let the emotions take over, as we had sports day to win. As I said earlier, all our houses had specific cheer songs, and the senior high schoolers came in especially ready that year. You know how you cheer until you lose your voice? Yeah, that was us that day. Granted, we still had to sit our senior exams in preparation for university, but the focus on that day was on sports. At least for me, it was.

Now, what I cannot remember is which house actually won; it was either yellow or green, I'm not sure. *But...*this sports day was different. It was our last one. You could have thought the school was one big house because the cheers that went up that day were like none others. We, the seniors, led in the cheering like no other time. The energy in the school was palpable. We didn't only autograph our books but our T-shirts and dresses, too. Oh, what a year that was!

I think about King Jehoshaphat and the men of Judah and Jerusalem as those houses we had in high school. The win for the king was the win for all.

Read 2 Chronicles 20: 27. In what state does it say that King Jehoshaphat, the men of Judah, and the men of Jerusalem returned?

_____

_____

_____

_____

_____

For what reason did they rejoice?

_____

_____

_____

_____

_____

Whom did they rejoice over?

_____

_____

_____

_____

_____

Let's write out Psalm 95:1–3.

"Come, let us sing for _____
to the _____; let
us shout aloud to the Rock of our salvation. Let us come before him with thanksgiving and _____
with_____ and _____. For
the _____, the great King above all
gods."

What a reassuring verse! Rejoice in your victory as the storm
is over.

In 2 Chronicles 20:27, we see the word "return." The word "return," as we know, means "to go back": the men and the king returned to Jerusalem. But from what we learned in verse 25, they
did not return empty-handed. See, the storm may have taken
you away or taken away from you; but in this verse, Jesus reas-

sures us that we shall get back what was taken away and that we will get back more than we lost.

When I think about the sentence "rejoice in the Lord," it reminds me of the four (or indefinite) part "round" we used to sing in Sunday school, "Rejoice in the Lord." There is something about rejoicing that is contagious and requires other people to join in and celebrate with you. King Jehoshaphat rejoiced with the people of Judah and Jerusalem.

If you are going through a storm right now, whom will you rejoice with (because you *will* rejoice)? If you went through a significant storm in the past, whom did you rejoice with? Whom would you rejoice with for any future storms that may come your way?

_____

_____

_____

_____

_____

_____

_____

Let's highlight some of the many verses in the Bible where we are instructed to rejoice. Read:

- Philippians 4:4
- Joel 2:23
- 1 Chronicles 16:10
- Romans 5:3–4
- Deuteronomy 12:7
- Psalm 32:11

Select some of the verses that you will commit to memory for this week as you remind yourself to rejoice in it all. You can write them out here:

_____
_____
_____
_____
_____

As we close today's study, let us do so with prayer:

Father, in the name of Your Son, Jesus, we come before You. We bless Your holy name. We thank You for giving us joy during and after the storm. We praise You for the victory, and like King Jehoshaphat and his men, rejoice, for You have given us cause to rejoice. Thank You for fighting this battle for us. For those who are still going through the storm, we ask, Father, that You give them Your strength and resilience to power through. We thank You for all that You are, Father. In Jesus's name, we pray. Amen.

What five things are you most grateful for today?

_____
_____
_____
_____
_____
_____
_____

AN ORCHESTRA

When we were young, our parents would take us to watch musicals. To date, I have always enjoyed going to watch plays, but musicals were the next level for me. There is something about a live band or orchestra, for that matter, that really brings the story to life. One favorite childhood play was the story of *Oliver Twist*, which, at the time, was being performed by a local high school. I think I watched the play three times because I enjoyed it so much. If you ever went early, during their rehearsals, you would hear them put voice to instrument in a perfect blend. They told of how powerful the instruments were that even without the vocalists, the essence of the song was felt.

In my opinion, instruments in a musical piece are the icing on the cake. It's no wonder that music is said to be a global language. For example, you may not know how to speak any African dialects, but once their drums beat, their stringed instruments are strung, the traditional dancers take to the stage; you can find yourself moving along to their melodious sounds with no knowledge of the words spoken.

Then there is the orchestra. Songs will typically have some instruments, but they mainly accompany the main instrument, which is the vocals, but an orchestra is different. It is predominantly the ensemble of the instruments accompanying each other in tandem. The orchestra, typically, will have an instrument from every family, so the sound that comes from the musical piece is a statement in and of itself.

In 2 Chronicles 20:25, we learned about the importance of going back to collect the gifts that the storm left. Then in 2 Chronicles 20:27, we saw about rejoicing and doing so with your comrades. Then, now in 2 Chronicles 20:28, we read about how they entered Jerusalem: "They entered Jerusalem _____ _____ with harps and lutes and trumpets."

Out of curiosity, I wanted to learn about the uniqueness of each of these instruments. I was curious to know why they would have chosen those specific instruments and to see if there is something we can glean from.

Harp. It is said to be in a family of its own, and unlike the piano, the harp uses specific music sheets. It is said to be one of the oldest instruments in the world. We can see that, given that King Jehoshaphat and his community were using it back then.

Lute. It always looks like a broken guitar with a rounded belly. However, any instrument that is plucked is considered to be the lute, including the violin, the western guitar, and the Indonesian rebab (a stringed instrument similar looking to the violin but played in an upright position).

Trumpet. It is known for how loud it is; it's often chosen for pieces where the volume is required, like in school bands and even army bands.

Looking at the various unique features of the instruments the king's people used as they went to the temple of the Lord, I do not wonder why they were selected for such an occasion. The combination of these instruments must've sounded like a philharmonic. The power and every note in place with the desired outcome, in the case of King Jehoshaphat and his men, were to bring home the victory.

In what ways do you celebrate the victories in your life?

_____

_____

_____

_____

What can you bring to the temple of the Lord?

_____

_____

_____

_____

As we close today, may you gather your instruments of jubilee for how far God has brought you.

What five things are you most grateful for today?

_____

_____

_____

_____

_____

_____

LET IT BE A LESSON (SWAHILI: *ILIWE FUNZO: E LEE WAY FOO N ZOW)*

The successful win of King Jehoshaphat's armies was a direct result of his obedience to God. As we have seen, God gave him specific instructions on what to do and what position to maintain for this specific fight. In its entirety, this way of fighting did not necessarily become a blueprint for other kings on how to fight because they, too, would be given specific instructions for their different battles. So, know this: in each battle you face, God will give you specific directions on how He wants you to participate. Before we highlight the specific instructions given to King Jehoshaphat, here are the general rules and prerequisites of how God fights for His children:

- God fights on behalf of His people.
- If you trust God, there is a glory that you receive by trusting Him. God wants us to trust Him even when it seems difficult.
- Praise before the battle: this cannot be underscored, for there is great power in your praise.

Every battle has its differences. In the battles you face, ask the Holy Spirit to give you specific instructions that are unique to that battle.

Let's look at the famous story of David and Goliath in 1 Samuel 17 and see what we can learn regarding specific tools used for his specific fight. Who was Goliath? Write down 1 Samuel 17:4–7 here:

"A _____ named Goliath, who was from Gath, came out of the Philistine camp. He was _____. He had a _____ on his head and wore a coat of scale armor weighing_____; on his legs he wore _____ and a _____ was slung on his back. His spear shaft was _____, and its iron point weighed _____. His _____ went ahead of him."

Isn't it the case that the challenge you are facing is always larger, scarier, seems undefeatable, more skilled or qualified? When we look at Goliath's stature, we see he surely was a much larger person than David. But as we have learned, who was fighting David's fight?

_____.

That's right; God was, just as in your family's situation: present your challenge to God and watch Him slay that issue for you.

Let's continue to read about David and Goliath. We see something very interesting happen in verses 38–40. Whose tunic did Saul dress David in?

_____

_____

_____

_____

_____

In verse 39, whose sword did David fasten over the tunic?

_____

_____

_____

_____

_____

What did he try and do?

_____

_____

_____

_____

_____

Why did he try to do this?

_____

_____

_____

_____

_____

Then, just at the end of verse 39, David says something to Saul.
What does he say?

_____

_____

_____

_____

_____

What was the reason he gave Saul?

_____

_____

_____

_____

_____

Did David still wear Saul's tunic?

_____

_____

_____

_____

_____

In verse 40, what does David do next?

_____

_____

_____

_____

_____

Could it be that we sometimes try to fight our battles the way others fought theirs? That you sometimes downplay our own skills, and yet you are made in the image and likeness of God, but you seem to doubt your abilities? Given his stature, even he, Goliath, mocked David, asking him in verse 43, "Am I a dog that you come at me with sticks?" What does David respond with in verse 45?

Write it down here:

"You come against me _____

_____

_____

_____

_____whom you have defied."

If we go back to verse 40, what do we learn that David packed instead in preparation for this fight?

_____

_____

_____

_____

_____

For the battle you and your family are facing, what do you have that "you are used to"? What skills, armor do you have that are unique to you?

_____

_____

_____

_____

_____

Using his stone and sling, what did David do to Goliath?

_____

_____

_____

_____

Both of these accounts of specific and general instructions, the victory David and King Jehoshaphat and their communities experienced, were not simply just good wins but rather lessons to the neighboring kingdoms. Friends, your victory is not yours alone. Those around you, your community, will know how God fought for you. They will learn, simply put, not to mess with you, for you have God on your side, and if that is how He fought for you, then yes, the "fear of God" will certainly come upon them.

When the Philistines in 1 Samuel 17: 51 saw that their hero, Goliath, was dead, what did they do?

_____

_____

_____

_____

In the same way, your enemies will turn and run once they see that you have defeated your "Goliath."

In 1 Samuel 17:52, what did the men of Israel and Judah do?

_____

_____

_____

_____

May your community surge toward your enemies to finish the job started, and may they also run toward you in victory and celebrations when God slays your "Goliath."

Remember we wrote down Isaiah 61:9? The last part of it reads, "All who see them [that is you] will acknowledge that they are a people the LORD has blessed" (text in brackets mine).

Isn't that amazing that God Himself will ensure that all who hear your story will fear the Lord? Second Chronicles 20:29 says that the fear of God came upon how many kingdoms?

_____
_____
_____
_____
_____

When did they get this fear?

_____
_____
_____
_____
_____

They don't even need to see you, have been there with you; just hearing about how the Lord fought for you will be enough to have them fearful.

We see a similar situation in Genesis 35:5. It states that when Jacob was returning to Bethel, God ensured his safety.

When did the terror of God fall upon all the towns around them?

_____

_____

_____

_____

_____

How many people pursued Jacob and his people?

_____

_____

_____

_____

_____

See, when God fights for you, even the potential pursuers will be filled with the fear of the Lord. Take that to the bank!

Every time God fights a battle, He ensures that a lesson is learned, that your enemies know that this one here is God's child and that they should not mess with him or her, but should they try...

We see yet another example of this in Deuteronomy 2:25. It says, "This very day I will begin to put the terror and fear of you on all the nations under heaven. They will hear reports of you and will tremble and will be in anguish because of you."

Underline this verse in your Bible. This is a battle like no other because the frontline soldier is Jesus: sit tight! Simply at the sound of your reports, the enemies will tremble. If that did not encourage you!

Exodus 14:14

Moses tells a group of scared Israelites not to be afraid as they were facing their enemies, the Egyptians, who were coming after them. In verse 14, what does he tell them the Lord will do?

_____

_____

_____

_____

But they needed only to do what?

_____

_____

_____

_____

_____

What does it say in Exodus 14:18?

_____

_____

_____

_____

_____

What does the last sentence in Exodus 14:25 state?

_____

_____

_____

_____

_____

They knew to step aside, for they realized who was fighting for them. And how many survived, as reported in Exodus 14:28?

_____

_____

_____

_____

_____

You need only to be still. He doesn't just start the job but gets it done and leaves a solid message behind.

This is a time, as good as any, to invite Jesus into your life if you haven't already. This is a great opportunity to get to know this Jesus on a personal level. It could be that you have pulled away from your faith, that some of the challenges in life have left you doubting His love for you. It is my hope that this study has re-ignited that knowledge that, indeed, He loves you more than you can ever know. If this is you, say this prayer, and let's invite Jesus into your life:

> *Dear Father,*
> *It's me; I come to You in the name of Jesus. I know I am a sin-ner. Today, I confess with my mouth and believe in my heart that You died on the cross for me and rose again. I ask You to come into my life, and I make You my Lord and Savior. Thank You for saving me. In Jesus's name, I pray. Amen!*

If this was your first time saying this prayer, contact your Bible study leader, your pastor, or a leader in the faith and let them know of this great decision you have just made, so they can give you direction and answer any questions you might have.

Also, read Ephesians, chapters 1 and 2, and see who God says that you are. Write those things down in your prayer journal as a constant reminder.

Let's close today's study in prayer.

Father God, we bless Your name. We thank You that You not only fight for us but send a clear message to those around us on who it was that was fighting on our behalf. We ask that You help us walk in obedience to You and have the courage to follow Your instructions. We cannot thank You enough. May Your name be glorified, and may those who do not know You get to know You and have a relationship with You so that they, too, do not live their lives without You. We praise You and honor You. In Jesus's name, we pray, amen.

What five things are you most grateful for today?

_____

_____

_____

_____

_____

_____

NOT JUST ON SOME SIDES, BUT ON EVERY SIDE

In the season when my family and I were faced with multiple armies, this story of King Jehoshaphat was one of the ones I clung to. We are a testimony of God fighting vast armies for us. We had so much coming against us that the victory of each and every battle gave the entire family hope. Whereas we always tried to keep our faith strong, it was the initial victory that gave us more wind under our sails to complete the remaining challenges. It gave us hope that the rest, too, would be won, and they were! The physical and emotional fatigue rendered us weak sometimes, but as it was in our season, God will restore your rest.

Friends, we have come to the end of this powerful story documented in 2 Chronicles 20:1–30. Before we learn today's lesson, let's take a look back at the previous weeks. Can you believe it has been six weeks already? In the spaces below, write down what has stuck with you throughout each week.

Week 1

_____

Week 2

_____

Week 3

_____

Week 4

_____

Week 5

_____

Week 6

_____

Which nuggets stood out for you most?

_____
_____
_____
_____
_____
_____
_____
_____

So, now we read the final verse of our study, 2 Chronicles 20:30. Write it down below:

_____

_____

_____

_____

_____

On what side did God give rest to King Jehoshaphat?

_____

_____

_____

_____

_____

It's not only the one thing you have been battling with that He will give you rest in. Regardless of what side the enemy was trying to come at you, He will give you rest. It says King Jehoshaphat was at peace. What a sigh of relief! See, the text does not state how long this fight took, but no matter how long it took, it ends with him being at peace on every side. What an ending!

Turn to 1 Chronicles 22:9. Here we see David speaking to his son, Solomon, and giving instructions on how he was chosen by God to build a temple. In this verse, he states that Solomon will be a man of what? "_____ and _____." And that God will give him what? "_____ from _____ on _____. His name will be Solomon and I will grant Israel peace and quiet during his reign."

In the same way, the fear of the Lord will be upon others simply by them learning about who fought for you.

In 2 Chronicles 20:30, who was at peace?

_____

_____

_____

_____

_____

And those who fought this battle with you: your family, your Bible study family, your friends, they too benefit from your victory. The peace of God will reign on them.

All those who were with you will encounter the same peace!

The verse says that God will give you rest. Let's take that in. Going through a storm is taxing, exhausting, unsettling, etc. You have had many a sleepless night, many a worry and cry, and just sheer fatigue. God is so loving that "every side" means that even your body gets a break. Sigh!

For example, you know that moment when you've been driving through a heavy rainstorm and your hands are tightly clenched around the steering wheel, your eyes exhausted from trying to see your way, and you finally make it home safe—that relief? Yeah, this is better.

Read Psalm 23:5–6.

In the King James Version of verse 5, it reads, "Thou preparest a table before me in the presence of mine enemies: thou anointest my head with oil; my cup runneth over."

The blessings of the Lord will be upon you and beside you and around you. You will be a blessing to those around you, for God has blessed you and you have trusted God.

Before listing down your final gratitude, turn to the back of the book and complete the road map together with your family. This road map is a quick reference to the thirty tools taught in this study: it allows you to glance at the tools to remind yourself of how to tackle any future battles.

Your final gratitude. What five things are you most grateful for today?

_____

_____

_____

_____

_____

_____

It is my hope that you continue listing your gratitudes every day. Gratitude is not only for when things are difficult or when things are good but for all seasons. Jesus reminds us in 1 Thessalonians 5:16–18, "Be joyful *always*: pray continually, *give thanks in all circumstances*, for this is God's will for you in Christ Jesus."

As you complete these six weeks of learning what to do when the storms of life blow, take Numbers 6:24–26 with you. May it bless you, and may you continue to be a blessing to those around you.

May "the LORD bless you and keep you; the LORD make his face to shine upon you and be gracious to you." May "the LORD turn his face toward you and give you peace" (Numbers 6:24–26).

Your Family Battle-Plan Model

This Bible study has given us thirty tactics on how to fight battles in our lives using God's way. Now, fill in the model below, culminating from each week's lessons (in summary) so that you can have a quick reference to remind yourself of them during future challenges.

_____

(Insert your name or family name here)

Victory Plan